NUTSHELLS

EQUITY AND TRUSTS
IN A NUTSHELL

Monica2hao

AUSTRALIA
Law Book Company
Sydney

CANADA and USA
Carswell
Toronto

HONG KONG
Sweet & Maxwell Asia

NEW ZEALAND
Brookers
Wellington

SINGAPORE and MALAYSIA
Sweet & Maxwell Asia
Singapore and Kuala Lumpur

NUTSHELLS

EQUITY AND TRUSTS IN A NUTSHELL

SIXTH EDITION

by

Michael Haley
Solicitor, Professor of Law
Keele University

Based on the original text by
Angela Sydenham

London • Sweet & Maxwell • 2004

First Edition 1987
Reprinted 1988
Reprinted 1990
Second Edition 1991
Third Edition 1994
Reprinted 1996
Fourth Edition 1997
Fifth Edition 2000
Reprinted 2002
Reprinted 2003
Sixth Edition 2004

Published in 2004 by Sweet & Maxwell Limited of
100 Avenue Road, London NW3 3PF
Typeset by LBJ Typesetting Ltd of Kingsclere
Printed in Great Britain by CPD Wales, Ebbw Vale

No natural forests were destroyed to make this product.
Only farmed timber was used and re-planted.

A CIP catalogue record for this book is available
from the British Library.

ISBN 0 421 871202

CONTENTS

1. AN INTRODUCTION TO EQUITY

Background

"Equity" is a term that invokes notions of good conscience, fairness and justice. In modern times, it exerts an influence in every aspect of the civil law (*e.g.* contract, tort and land law). Originally, equity was the name given to the branch of law that was administered by the Court of Chancery. It developed to counter the injustice caused by the rigidity of the writ system that operated in the common law courts. Put simply, if there was no writ, then there was no cause of action upon which a claimant could rely. In such instances, the aggrieved party might apply to the King for justice. The King, in turn, passed on these appeals to the Lord Chancellor. In time, the Lord Chancellor developed his own court, the Court of Chancery. Initially, the Court of Chancery operated in a flexible manner in the dispensation of justice. Inevitably, however, equity developed its own body of rules that had, by the nineteenth century, become almost as technical and rigid as those at common law.

Not surprisingly, a dual system of courts proved to be expensive, cumbersome and inconvenient. The Judicature Acts 1873–75 addressed this issue and provided that all courts could exercise an equitable jurisdiction alongside the common law jurisdiction. Although the Acts merged the Court of Chancery with the common law courts (to form the Supreme Court of Judicature), it did not fuse the two streams of law. The Acts did establish, however, the supremacy of equity by providing that, if there is a conflict between law and equity, the equitable rules will prevail.

Equity's impact

There are many and varied contributions to the modern law that have been made by equity. The following provide the major examples:

(a) *the trust* **(originally called a "use").** If property was conveyed to "A upon trust for B" the common law courts regarded A as the absolute owner and would not recognise B's rights. Equity, however, would enforce the trust and compel A (as trustee) to hold the property on behalf of B (the beneficiary);

(b) *restrictive covenants.* The general rule is that covenants only bind the parties themselves and do not bind third parties. Although the benefit of a covenant can easily be transferred to a third party expressly or under statute (*e.g.* the Contracts (Rights of Third Parties) Act 1999), stricter rules govern its burden. In relation to freehold covenants affecting land, equity stepped in to allow restrictive (or negative) covenants to run with the land so as to bind all future purchasers;

(c) *the mortgagor's equitable right to redeem.* Where a landowner mortgages his land (*i.e.* offers the land as security for a loan), the mortgage contract will specify a contractual date for redemption. This is the agreed date when the debt is to be paid off (redeemed) by the borrower. At common law, the borrower had to discharge the loan by this date or he would lose the land. Equity intervened and allowed repayment to be made even though the contractual date had passed;

(d) *the subpoena.* This is an order developed by the Court of Chancery to compel a litigant to appear in person before the court and to be questioned;

(e) *estoppel.* An estoppel arises in circumstances where X makes a statement, promise or some other representation to Y and, as a result, Y acts to his detriment. Y's detrimental reliance can trigger an estoppel that will prevent X from enforcing his strict legal rights. Of the various categories of estoppel that exist, the most commonly found are promissory estoppel and proprietary estoppel. Promissory estoppel can only be employed as a defence (it is a shield and not a sword) and hinges upon there being a promise as to future conduct (not existing fact). Proprietary estoppel requires a statement (whether in the present or future tense) concerning land and can be used as a cause of action (*i.e.* it confers a positive right to sue);

(f) *new remedies.* Remedies at law were limited to recovery of the property or damages. A wider range of remedies was introduced by equity. These include specific performance, injunctions, rectification (rewriting of a contract), rescission (unilateral withdrawal from a contract) and the appointment of a receiver (to receive income from a business). Until the Chancery Amendment Act 1858, however, equity could not award damages for breach of contract. The Act (now in its modern form of s.50 of the Supreme Court Act 1981) allowed an award of damages either in addition or in substitution for an injunction or specific performance. A distinguishing feature of all equitable remedies is that they are discretionary (*i.e.* not available as of right) and appropriate only where the common law remedies are inadequate. The remedies of specific performance and injunction are considered in more detail below.

The maxims of equity

There are a number of maxims that represent the general principles of equity. These maxims retain importance because they provide broad guidelines by which the courts exercise their equitable jurisdiction. They should always be borne in mind because, as equitable remedies are discretionary, they may often dictate when (and when not) a remedy will be granted. The most important equitable maxims include:

(a) *equity will not suffer a wrong without a remedy.* This is not to be taken too literally as equitable remedies are geared only to strike against unconscionable behavior and operate only if that behavior constitutes a legal (as opposed to a mere moral) wrongdoing. The law of trusts provides a good illustration where equity (but not the common law) allows the beneficiary to enforce his rights. More modern developments include the giving of an equity in the matrimonial home to a deserted spouse, the evolution of promissory estoppel, the employment of the constructive trust, expanding the range of injunctions and the extension of liability for breach of confidence;

(b) *he who seeks equity must do equity.* This looks to the *future* conduct of the claimant and entails that, for example, if the claimant seeks to rescind (*i.e.* withdraw from) a contract, the court will ensure that the claimant acts equitably by returning any deposit paid under the contract. Similarly, if the claimant seeks to specifically enforce a contract then he must be prepared to perform his side of the bargain. The maxim is, therefore, employed to ensure fairness;

(c) *he who comes to equity must come with clean hands.* This looks to the *past* conduct of the claimant and entails that, if the claimant's conduct in relation to the dispute has been improper, the chances are that equity will not assist him. For example, specific performance will not be granted in relation to a contract which was brought about by the claimant's misrepresentation or fraud or where the claimant is himself in breach of that contract;

(d) *delay defeats equity.* This is sometimes called "laches" and means that a claimant who takes too long to exercise his legal rights will not receive the assistance of equity. The idea is that the claimant has to act expeditiously. In practice, the role of this maxim has been subsumed by the Limitation Acts (which set out time limits within which actions must be commenced), but it still exerts influence when deciding whether equitable remedies should be granted;

(e) *equity is equality.* This maxim applies where two or more persons claim to be interested in the same property. If their respective shares are not stated, and in the absence of a contrary intention, equity assumes that they are to have equal shares;

(f) *equity will not assist a volunteer.* Equity will not grant specific performance of a gratuitous promise (*i.e.* an agreement that is not supported by consideration). In relation to trusts, this means that equity will assist a beneficiary only when there is a perfectly constituted trust (*i.e.* once legal title to the trust property has vested in the trustee). This is considered further in Ch.6;

(g) *equity looks on that as done that ought to be done.* This maxim is well demonstrated in *Walsh v Lonsdale* (1882) where a seven-year lease was granted to the tenant, but no deed was executed. The fixed term lease was, therefore, equitable. In the light that specific performance of the contract to create a legal lease was available, the court admitted that an equitable lease is as good as a legal lease. This was because equity looked on the lease as "legal" as soon as it was informally created. Another example of this maxim is the "doctrine of conversion" that arises on a binding contract for the sale of land. As soon as the contract is entered, the vendor becomes the trustee of the legal estate for the benefit of the purchaser. This entails that the vendor's interest has been "converted" into the agreed proceeds of sale. Accordingly, if the property is damaged after the contract, the risk potentially falls on the shoulders of the purchaser and the vendor is entitled to the full purchase price;

(h) *equity will not permit a statute to be used as an engine of fraud.* This prevents a party from relying upon an absence of statutory formalities (*e.g.* relating to land contracts, the creation of legal leases and express trusts and the registration of land charges) if to do so would be unconscionable and unfair. In *Shah v Shah* (2001), a deed was not properly executed and a witness to the deed sought to have it set aside for his own benefit. The court held that for the witness to rely on this defect would be tantamount to fraud and upheld the deed;

(i) *equity acts in personam.* This means that equitable remedies are personal in that they are exercised against specific persons. They compel or permit a person to do something or not to do something. For example, in relation to a breach of trust the remedy is exercisable against the trustees personally. This can involve an order freezing the trustees' assets even if those assets are subject to a foreign jurisdiction. The maxim also entails that an individual, who does not comply with an order of the court, will be held to be in contempt and may be imprisoned until he purges his contempt;

(j) *equity imputes an intention to fulfil an obligation.* This means that where a person is obliged to do something, but instead does something else that could be regarded as a performance of the obligation, equity will regard this as fulfilling the obligation. This is the basis of the doctrines of "performance" and "satisfaction".

Performance and satisfaction

Examples of "performance" include an unfulfilled covenant in a marriage settlement to purchase and settle land where a contract to purchase land was subsequently made (*Lord Lochmere v Lady Lochmere* (1733)) and a covenant to leave money where the covenantee was entitled to the money on the covenantor's intestacy (*Blandy v Whitmore* (1732)).

An example of "satisfaction" is the satisfaction of a debt by a legacy. If a person leaves a legacy to a person to whom he owes a debt then it may be that the debt will be satisfied by the legacy. The will may make it clear whether this is the intention. If not, a presumption of satisfaction will apply provided the debt was incurred before the will was made; the legacy is as large or larger than the debt, and the will does not contain a direction to pay debts. Conversely a legacy may be cancelled by a lifetime gift as in *Re Cameron (deceased)* (1999) where a lifetime gift to a grandson for his education cancelled out a legacy under the grandmother's will.

Specific performance

Specific performance is, put simply, a court order requiring a party to a contract to perform his side of the bargain. When granted this will be either as an alternative or in addition to damages for breach of contract.

(a) *General principles.* This remedy will not be granted if damages would adequately compensate the claimant. An example of where specific performance will be readily granted concerns contracts for the sale of land. This is because each piece of land is considered to be unique and damages would not compensate the potential purchaser. Although damages may be suitable for the vendor, a need for mutuality (see below) will enable him instead to obtain specific performance of a land contract. An action for a specific performance, moreover, may be commenced even before there has been an actual breach of contract. This would arise where there is an anticipatory breach (*e.g.* the one party states that he will not perform the contract): see *Hasham v Zenab* (1960).

(b) *Specific performance is not available for*:

(i) contracts for the sale of goods unless they are unique (*Behnke v Bede Shipping Company* (1927): a ship) or where special circumstances make the payment of damages inadequate (*Sky Petroleum Ltd v VIP Petroleum Ltd* (1974): sale of petrol at a time of world shortage);

(ii) illegal or immoral contracts (*e.g.* a contract to pay for stolen goods);

(iii) agreements without consideration ("equity will not assist a volunteer");

(iv) contracts for transient interests (*e.g.* a tenancy at will). Specific performance may, however, be available to enforce contractual licences (*Verrall v Great Yarmouth* (1981));

(v) partnership agreements, unless the parties have already begun to act on their agreement;

(vi) contracts involving personal services (*e.g.* an agreement by an actor to appear in a play);

(vii) contracts requiring continuous supervision (*e.g.* a contract to provide porterage in a block of flats);

(viii) contracts to pay money;

(ix) contracts to exercise a testamentary power of appointment;

(x) contracts to sell goodwill independently of the business to which it adheres;

(xi) contracts to refer a dispute to arbitration;

(xii) contracts to build. In *Wolverhampton Corporation v Emmons* (1901), however, the court held that a construction contract could be specifically enforced where the work was sufficiently defined in the contract, damages would be inadequate and the defendant had already taken possession of the land on which the work was to be carried out.

(c) *Defences to specific performance.* Even though the contract may be of a type that is suitable for specific performance, the defendant may be able to invoke a defence to the claim. These include where:

(i) specific performance of only part of the contract is sought;

(ii) there has been some misrepresentation or other default by the claimant (the "clean hands" maxim);

(iii) the contract reflects a common mistake shared by the parties;

(iv) there is some misdescription in the contract of the property to be transferred;

(v) there has been an unreasonable lapse of time ("laches") in seeking the order;

(vi) it will cause hardship to the parties or to a third party;

(vii) the claimant has a defective or dubious title to the subject matter of the contract. The court will not force a doubtful title on a purchaser;

(viii) there is a want of mutuality, *i.e.* where the remedy is not available to the other party. For example, where one party is below the age of majority.

Injunctions

(a) Injunctions are a discretionary remedy. Damages may be awarded in lieu of or in addition to an injunction. An injunction may be granted against a class or organisation restraining the unlawful acts of unidentified people. A person may seek an injunction to protect his existing private rights. Public rights are usually protected by injunctions obtained by the Attorney General. A local authority may also seek an injunction to protect public rights in the locality or to enforce planning control. To act in breach of an injunction is contempt of court.

(b) There are various types of injunction each of which has been designed to achieve a different function. These categories include:

   (i) *the prohibitory injunction.* This is an injunction which forbids the party to do or to continue to do an unlawful act (*e.g.* to build upon land in breach of a restrictive covenant);

   (ii) *the mandatory injunction.* This is an order that an act be undone (*e.g.* to demolish a building which has been built in breach of a restrictive covenant). Hence, a mandatory injunction when granted is likely to undo a wrongful act rather than to order the defendant to carry out a positive obligation. This is because of the difficulties of supervision: *Gravesham Borough Council v British Railways Board* (1978). Mandatory injunctions are not common;

   (iii) *the perpetual injunction.* This is an injunction which is in final settlement of the dispute between the parties and is issued at the completion of the court proceedings;

   (iv) *the interim injunction* (sometimes known as an inter-locutory junction). This is an injunction which is made during the course of legal proceedings and which is effective only until the eventual trial of the action. It is designed to restrain the defendant immediately without waiting for a full court hearing;

   (v) *the without notice injunction.* This is an injunction granted in an emergency without the other side having been informed or given the opportunity to attend the hearing of the application;

(vi) *the quia timet injunction.* This is an injunction that is designed to prevent an anticipatory infringement of the claimant's rights where an infringement is realistic threat;

(vii) *a search order* (formerly known as an Anton Pillar order). This is an injunction that authorises the claimant to enter the defendant's premises to inspect and seize documents relevant to the case. The aim is to protect evidence in relation to impending litigation;

(viii) *a freezing injunction* (formerly known as a Mareva injunction). This is an injunction that prevents the defendant from removing his assets out of the jurisdiction of the court before the completion of litigation.

Guidelines for interim injunctions

(a) A series of guidelines as to when interim injunctions should be granted were set out by Lord Diplock in *American Cyanamid Co v Ethicon Ltd* (1975). These are:

(i) the claimant's case must not be frivolous or vexatious and there must be a serious question to be tried;

(ii) the "balance of convenience" test must be satisfied. This test involves weighing up the potential harm suffered by the applicant if no injunction is awarded with the potential inconvenience caused to the defendant if it is granted. For example, in *Gregory v Castleoak Ltd* (2002), the loss to the claimant, if the injunction was not granted, was minimal whereas, if granted, it would be financially disastrous for the defendant. The case for an injunction will be strengthened if the claimant is prepared to give an undertaking to the court to compensate the defendant for loss in the event of the eventual litigation being unsuccessful. If the claimant cannot afford to pay such potential damages, the court may refuse to order the injunction;

(iii) only as a last resort will the strength of each party's case be considered. Nevertheless, in *Series 5 Software v Clarke* (1996) more emphasis was placed upon this last guideline. The claimant's case was weak and, in refusing to grant injunctive relief, Laddie J. adopted a flexible approach. He was not prepared to relegate the strength of each party's case to the last resort.

(b) There are, however, exceptions to the *American Cyanamid* guidelines. They do not apply, for example, to trade disputes, cases involving public rights and applications for interim mandatory injunctions where the trial of this action is unlikely and where there is no arguable defence. In relation to breach of confidence cases, the court must have regard to the competing rights to privacy and freedom of expression contained in the Human Rights Act 1998: *Douglas v Hello* (2003).

Damages in lieu of an injunction

The general presumption is that, if a right is infringed, an injunction will be granted. In certain circumstances, however, the courts may award damages instead of injunctive relief. Following *Shelfer v City of London Electric Lighting Co Ltd* (1895), the working rule emerges that damages may be an alternative where:

(i) the claimant's loss is small;
(ii) the loss can be valued in money terms;
(iii) money would provide the claimant with adequate compensation; or
(iv) an injunction would be oppressive, unduly harsh or disproportionate.

For example, in *Jaggard v Sawyer* (1995) the claimant was granted damages rather than an injunction preventing access along a private roadway to a new house that would otherwise have been landlocked. The trespass caused little injury to the claimant and the loss could be easily estimated in monetary terms. The court believed that it would be oppressive to grant the injunction sought. Although in *Ludlow Music v Robbie Williams* (2000) the compensation payable was likely to be substantial, the court refused an injunction to restrain a breach of copyright. The reasoning was that it would be oppressive to allow the claimant to stop the sale of the album on which the offending song appeared. In *Daniells v Mendonca* (1999), however, the court granted a mandatory injunction for the removal of a building extension which involved a trespass on a neighbour's land. Here the claimant could not be adequately compensated by the small monetary payment that was likely to be awarded (see also *Nelson v Nicholson* (2000)).

Search order

This is an order preventing disposal by the defendant of any evidence prior to trial. It is especially important in commercial cases involving breach of confidence, copyright and passing off. Before an order will be made the following conditions must be met:

(i) there must be a strong prima facie case;
(ii) the claimant must show actual or potential damage of a serious nature; and
(iii) there must be clear evidence that the defendant has incriminating documents or other items that it is likely will be destroyed before the trial.

Guidelines on the execution of search orders were laid down in *Universal Thermosensors Ltd v Hibben* (1992). Although later overruled on a different ground, the guidelines remain valid. First, a search order should normally be executed in office hours when the defendant's solicitor could be present. Secondly, that a list of documents should be prepared before they are removed and the defendant given the opportunity to check them. Thirdly, where it is likely that a woman will be alone at the premises the party serving the order should be, or be accompanied by, a woman.

Freezing injunctions

These were originally granted where a claimant had brought an action in Britain against a foreign defendant who had assets within the jurisdiction that he might remove. It is now also possible to seek a freezing injunction where proceedings are started outside Britain.

In *Third Chandris Shipping Corporation v Unimarine SA* (1979) Lord Denning set out guidelines as to when a freezing injunction should be ordered. He suggested that the claimant should establish a good case by providing:

(i) a full and frank disclosure of all material matters;

(ii) particulars of his claim against the defendant and the points made against it by the defendant;

(iii) reasons for believing the defendant has assets within the jurisdiction;

(iv) grounds for believing that the assets may be removed or dissipated before the claim is satisfied; and

(v) an undertaking that, if the litigation subsequently fails, the defendant will be compensated.

The court has claimed a modern jurisdiction to grant such an injunction covering worldwide assets: see *Derby v Weldon* (1990). This power arises under s.37(1) of the Supreme Court Act 1981. Where a worldwide injunction is sought, there must usually be shown to be exceptional circumstances which justify the order. In *Re Bank of Credit and Commerce International (No.9)* (1994), for example, such an order was made to cater for "the complex international nature of the financial dealings". Before making this type of order, the court should be watchful that the defendant is not harshly treated and exposed to multiple litigation in the jurisdictions where the assets are held.

2. DESCRIPTIONS AND CLASSIFICATIONS OF TRUSTS

What is a trust?

Many attempts have been made to define the term "trust", but none as yet have been wholly successful. A trust is, therefore, easier to describe than to define. Although trusts come in a variety of forms and cater for different types of property and purpose, they all share the same essential characteristics. At its heart, a trust involves the fragmentation of legal title (legal ownership) and equitable title (beneficial ownership). The legal title is vested in a character known as the "trustee" and the trustee holds the trust property on behalf of the "beneficiary". It is only on this separation of title that equitable title assumes importance because the general rule is that legal title carries with it all rights: *Westdeutsche Landesbank Girocentrale v London Islington BC* (1996).

As will become clear, sometimes the trustees and the beneficiaries are the same people. This is likely to arise, for example, in relation to trusts of land. The trustee owes a "fiduciary" duty (*i.e.* a duty of utmost good faith) to both the settlor and the beneficiary. The entitlement of the beneficiaries will normally be set out in the document creating the trust (the "trust instrument"), but where this is not the case the rights of the beneficiaries can be implied by equity. Trusts can be of any sort of property: land, money, chattels, cheques and debts, etc.

Trusts distinguished from other concepts

1. *Bailment*. This is a common law relationship which arises when goods owned by A are, with A's permission, in the possession of B. This may be a contractual relationship (*e.g.* if you leave your car in a secure airport car park while on holiday) or a gratuitous relationship (*e.g.* when you store furniture in a relative's attic). This is very different from a trust because there is no transfer of ownership involved and the duties expected of the bailee are much less extensive than those expected from a trustee.

2. *Agency*. The relationship between principal and agent is normally contractual (*i.e.* you normally employ an agent, such as a solicitor or surveyor, to act on your behalf). The agent's job is to represent his principal's interests in dealings with third parties. An agent will not usually have title to the property vested in him, which means that, even if the agent has possession of goods, he will have no claim to ownership.

3. *Contract*. Trusts and contracts are very different creatures:

(a) a contract is a common law, personal obligation resulting from a negotiated agreement between the parties. A trust arises from equity and confers property rights (rights *in rem*) on the beneficiary that can be enforced against both the property itself and third parties;

(b) a contract is valid only if supported by consideration or made by deed. A beneficiary under a properly constituted trust, however, can enforce trust even though he has not given any consideration;

(c) a contract cannot usually be enforced by third parties ("privity of contract" is necessary). This rule is, however, subject to certain statutory exceptions as, for example, contained in the Contracts (Rights of Third Parties) Act 1999 and s.56 of the Law of Property Act 1925. In contrast, a beneficiary can always enforce a trust even if he is not a party to the agreement that created the trust.

4. Debt.   A debt is usually contractual (*e.g.* when I agree to repay a loan to my bank). It is a personal obligation whereas the interest of a beneficiary under a trust is a proprietary right. This distinction becomes clear on the insolvency of the person in whom the property is vested. If a trust is in existence, the trust property will not be available to the trustee's creditors. Where there is no trust, any creditor will be able to claim against the bankrupt's estate. This is illustrated in two classic cases:

(a) in *Barclays Bank Ltd v Quistclose Investments Ltd* (1970), Rolls Razor Ltd declared a dividend on shares which it could not pay. Quistclose agreed to make a loan specifically for the purpose of paying the dividends. The money was paid into a special account at Barclays Bank. Rolls then went into liquidation, leaving a large overdraft at Barclays. The Bank laid claim to the money in the special account in order to discharge the overdraft. The House of Lords held that, as Quistclose had paid the money for a particular purpose, on the failure of that purpose the Bank held the money on an implied trust for Quistclose. This is an example of a "resulting trust". The Bank was not, therefore, entitled to the money. The fact that there was a contract for a loan from Quistclose did not exclude the implication of a trust;

(b) in *Re Kayford Ltd* (1975), a mail order company opened a special "Customers' Trust Deposit Account" at its bank for advance payments received from its customers. This money was not available to its liquidator when the company was subsequently wound up. By opening the account, the company demonstrated the intention to create a trust of the prepayments in favour of its customers. The obligations were transferred from debt to trust. The money was not, therefore, available to its general creditors.

5. Gifts.   A transfer by way of gift involves an absolute transfer of title to the property concerned. For example, if I hand you £20 for your birthday, once the money is physically passed between us I cannot later insist that you pay it back. The money is unconditionally yours. If, instead, I hand you £20 and tell you to give it to X when you next see him then very different considerations apply. I (the settlor) have created a trust whereby you (the trustee) hold the money on trust for X (the beneficiary). It is not yours to keep and, if you spend it, you can be personally liable to account for its loss.

6. *Powers of appointment.* A power is discretionary and permissive whereas a trust is imperative and mandatory. An example of a power of appointment is where a trust is set up and the trustee is given the power to donate up to £500 to charity. If this power was not given, any donation would be unauthorised and in breach of trust. This power, therefore, allows the trustee lawfully to siphon some of the trust fund away from the beneficiaries. It is, however, purely up to the trustee to decide whether or not to give any money to charity. The trustee must, however, address his mind to whether or not to exercise the power.

The distinction between a power and a trust is important, but is not always easy to draw. For example, in *Burroughs v Philcox* (1840) a testator left property to his two children for their lives. He gave to the survivor of them a power to dispose of the property by will, "amongst my nephews and nieces or their children, either all to one of them, or to as many of them as my surviving child should think proper". It was held that this evinced a general intention to benefit a class and that, if the power of selection was not exercised, a trust had been created in favour of the nephews and nieces. As the surviving child failed to exercise the power, the property was divided equally amongst the beneficiaries. By way of contrast, in *Re Weeks's Settlement* (1897) a wife left property to her husband with a power "to dispose of all such property by will amongst our children". The court held that this power evinced no certainty of intention to create a trust and, therefore, the money had been given to the husband absolutely.

The major differences between powers and trusts are:

(i) a power can be legal (as with a power of attorney) or equitable. Trusts are always equitable;

(ii) a power is discretionary whereas a trust imposes a duty. Accordingly, if a trustee does not carry out his duties the court will intervene and compel him to do so. The court will not intervene to compel a person to exercise a power;

(iii) unlike the beneficiary under a trust, a potential beneficiary under a power has no interest in the property before
the power is exercised;

(iv) the rule of certainty of objects (considered in Ch.3) was
once different for powers than for trusts. Prior to *McPhail
v Doulton* (1971), all trustees would need a full list of
potential beneficiaries before they could carry out their
duties. This was unnecessary where someone had only a
power. It was sufficient if it could be said of any given
individual that he or she was or was not within the class
of objects specified by the donor of the power. The rule
for powers has now been extended to discretionary trusts.
The old complete list rule still applies to fixed trusts;

(v) if a donee of a power makes no appointments the
property reverts, as appropriate, either to the settlor or
stays in the trust fund.

7. Wills and intestacy.

(a) The relationship between a personal representative of a
deceased and a person entitled under a will (or the
intestacy rules) is similar to the relationship that exists
between trustee and beneficiary. Indeed, most of the
provisions of the Trustees Act 1925 apply in all these
situations, as does Pt I of the Trusts of Land and Appointment of Trustees Act 1996.

(b) Where a testator leaves a will appointing an "executor",
the executor will (according to the size of the deceased's
estate) obtain a grant of probate from the Probate Registry
of the High Court. Although the executor's powers relate
back to the testator's death, his ability to deal with the
assets of the deceased is often limited until the time
probate is granted. Where the deceased has left no will,
an "administrator" will be appointed by the Probate
Registry to deal with the estate. The administrator's
powers come from being granted letters of administration.

(c) The job of executors and administrators, both often
referred to as "personal representatives", is to wind up
and distribute the deceased's estate. The job of trustees is
to hold property on behalf of the beneficiaries.

(d) Until the personal representatives assent to the property
vesting in those entitled under the will or intestacy, they
hold both the legal and beneficial interest in the property.

In a trust, it is the beneficiaries alone who have the beneficial interest in the property.

(e) Under the Limitation Act 1980, claims to the personal estate of the deceased are statute-barred after 12 years. A beneficiary, however, only has six years to claim against a trustee for breach of trust. Neither time limit applies where there has been fraud or where the personal representative or trustee retains the property or has converted it to his own use.

(f) Whereas one of several personal representatives can dispose of personal property, trustees must always act jointly.

(g) Personal representatives can be appointed only by the will or by the court. New trustees, however, can be appointed by persons specified in the trust instrument (or given that power under the Trustee Act 1925) or following a direction given by beneficiaries under the Trusts of Land and Appointment of Trustees Act 1996.

Classification of trusts

As different writers classify trusts in different ways, there is no universal agreement upon what is always the proper classification. Nevertheless, the following categorisations reflect the conventional understanding:

1. Private and public trusts. A *private trust* is a trust for the benefit of either a named individual (*e.g.* "£50,000 to be held on trust for John") or a named class of individuals (*e.g.* "£50,000 to be held on trust for my children"). Private trusts can be fixed or discretionary in nature. They cannot, however, be used to advance a purpose because there is no one to enforce the trust. Subject to some odd exceptions, there is no such thing as a private purpose trust (sometimes called "a trust of imperfect obligation"). Hence, a trust to promote duck shooting (not being charitable) will fail. A *public trust* is a trust that is to benefit charity. This can be to benefit a named charitable organisation or to promote a charitable purpose (*e.g.* "£50,000 to relieve poverty in Africa"). Public purpose trusts are enforceable by the Attorney General.

2. Express trusts. These are trusts intentionally created either by the settlor expressly declaring himself to be a trustee or by transferring the property to a third party trustee to hold on stipulated trusts. Further sub-classifications of express trusts emerge:

   (a) completely and incompletely constituted trusts. This refers to the requirement that the trustee must have legal title to the trust property. If an owner of property declares himself to be a trustee of that property, there is no problem. He already has legal title. If a third party is the nominated trustee, however, it is necessary that legal title be transferred to that person. The precise method of transfer to be adopted depends upon what type of property is the subject matter of the trust. If the trustee does not have legal title, the trust is incompletely constituted and is not enforceable;

   (b) fixed trusts. A fixed trust is in contrast to a discretionary trust and is a trust where the beneficiaries and their shares are fixed (*i.e.* stipulated) by the settlor. For example, "£50,000 to be divided equally between Jack and Jill";

   (c) discretionary trusts. A discretionary trust takes its name from the fact that the settlor gives the trustee the discretion to select who, from a given class of person, will receive the trust property and, normally, in what shares. For example, "£50,000 to be divided between such of my children as my trustee shall nominate";

   (d) secret trusts. These are express trusts that are created by testamentary disposition (*i.e.* by will). Secret trusts can be "fully secret" or "half secret" in nature. A "fully secret" trust arises where, on the face of the will, X appears to leave an unconditional legacy to Y, but Y had previously agreed with X to hold the property on trust for Z. Note that the will makes no reference whatsoever to the existence of the trust. A "half secret" trust arises where the will makes express reference to the existence of a trust, but does not disclose the terms of that trust. An example would be where by will X bequeaths "£100,000 to Y on trusts that I have previously communicated to Y".

3. Implied trusts. These are trusts which were not expressly created and which arise by implication or by operation of law. The term may refer to resulting trusts, constructive trusts and trusts imposed by statute. The boundaries between resulting trusts and constructive trusts are not, however, always clear.

(a) *Resulting trusts.* A resulting trust may arise in two situations. First where an express trust fails for some reason (*e.g.* the beneficiaries are uncertain), the property will result back to the settlor or his estate. This is sometimes called an "automatic resulting trust". Secondly, where there is what is called a "presumed intention resulting trust" that will arise when, for example, X purchases a house, but legal title to it is registered in Y's name. In this case, Y will hold the property on resulting trust for X.

(b) *Constructive trusts.* In certain circumstances, equity will presume that a legal owner of property will hold that property on trust for another. These are trusts that are imposed irrespective of subjective intentions of the parties and operate where it would be unjust for the holder of the property to hold it for his own benefit. The traditional basis of the constructive trust is to prevent fraud, but in modern times the constructive trust is utilised whenever justice and good conscience requires it. A constructive trust is invoked in a variety of situations, for example, in relation to mutual wills, fully secret trusts, acquisition of the family home, unauthorised profits made by a trustee and the doctrine of conversion on a specifically enforceable contract.

(c) *Statutory trusts.* The classic example of a statutory trust arises in relation to the co-ownership of land. Co-ownership must always occur behind a trust and this may be under either a strict settlement or Settled Land Act trust (no new ones can be created after January 1, 1997) or, more commonly, a trust of land under the Trusts of Land and Appointment of Trustees Act 1996.

---

3. THE THREE CERTAINTIES

Due to the onerous duties placed upon a trustee, it is necessary that the settlor makes clear that a trust was intended, what property is subject to the trust and who the beneficiaries are so that the trust can be enforced. Accordingly, the law has developed a test known as the "three certainties" that encompasses certainty of intention, certainty of subject matter and certainty of objects. These requirements were specified by Lord Langdale M.R. in *Knight v Knight* (1840). Except as to charitable trusts which do not need certainty of objects (see below), the three certainties need to be present so that a trust can be workable and capable of supervision by the court.

Certainty of intention

There is no magic formula necessary to show the intention to create a trust. Equity looks to the intent rather than to the form. Although desirable, the use of the word "trust" is not essential. Even if the term is employed, this is no guarantee that a trust will be discerned: *Midland Bank v Wyatt* (1995).

1. Precatory words. Precatory words are words merely of hope and desire, *e.g.* "in the hope that", "I would like that", "I desire that" and "I feel confident that". Although in the older cases precatory words were sometimes sufficient to create a trust, this is no longer the case. The court is now looking for imperative words that impose a mandatory obligation on the trustee. A moral obligation is not enough: *Sweeney v Coghill* (1998). If there is doubt, the burden lies on the claimant to establish the necessary intention on a balance of probabilities: *Re Snowden* (1979).

For example, in *Lambe v Eames* (1871) the testator gave his estate to his widow "to be at her disposal in any way she thinks best for the benefit of herself and her family". It was held that these were precatory words and did not create a trust. No certainty of intention to create a trust was found in *Re Adams and the Kensington Vestry* (1884). There the gift was made "in full confidence that she will do what is right as to the disposal thereof between my children either in her lifetime or by will after her decease". Similarly, in *Margulies v Margulies* (1998) provision for the testator's brother and sister "if considered in the interests of family harmony" did not evince sufficient certainty of intention to create a trust.

There are two decisions that, at first glance, seem to contradict the modern rule that precatory words will not create a trust. In *Comiskey v Bowring-Hanbury* (1905), the House of Lords held that in looking for certainty of words or intention one should construe the document as a whole. There a testamentary gift to the widow "in full confidence" that she leave the property on her death to one or more of his nieces did not prevent the creation of a trust in favour of the nieces. This is because the settlor went on to make what is called "a gift over in default of appointment". The added words that proved crucial were, "in default of any disposition by her . . . I hereby direct that all my estate and property acquired by her under my will shall at her death be equally divided among my nieces". The imperative wording of the gift over imposed the mandatory obligation on the widow. This case should not, therefore, be cited as authority for saying that precatory words can constitute a trust. In *Re Steele's Will Trusts* (1948), a solicitor drafted a trust for his client that followed an outmoded precedent which featured precatory words. Although this may have worked in the past to create a trust, it should have failed for a lack of certainty of intention. Nevertheless, the court concluded that the deliberate use of the precedent (albeit itself defective) demonstrated the necessary intention. This is a maverick case that turns upon its own facts and is, probably, unsound.

2. Declaration of a trust. As mentioned no special words are necessary to create a trust and a trust may be found even where there is no document. The intention can be derived from spoken words or conduct.

(a) In *Paul v Constance* (1977) there was found to be a trust where Mr Constance said to Ms Paul about his bank account, "the money is as much yours as mine". This was not a gift, but was instead a declaration of a trust that gave Ms Paul an equal share in the bank account. This should be contrasted with *Jones v Lock* (1865) where a father held out a cheque, which was payable to him, in front of his child and said "I give this to baby". This was a failed gift (the title to the cheque did not pass) and could not be construed as a declaration of trust.

(b) In *Barclays Bank v Quistclose* (1970), an implied trust was created by the paying of money (borrowed specifically to pay dividends to shareholders) into a separate bank account. In *Re Kayford* (1975) advance payments made by customers were placed into a "Customers' Trust Deposit Account" and this again evidenced the intention to create a trust.

(c) A similar approach was recently adopted by the House of Lords in *Twinsectra v Yardley* (2002) where a solicitor received money from a lender (Twinsectra) on behalf of a client. The solicitor gave the undertaking that the money would be used only for the purposes of purchasing property for his client and that the loan would be repaid with interest. This was held to remain Twinsectra's money until the acquisition of property in accordance with the solicitor's undertaking. Lord Millett described this as,

> " . . . an entirely orthodox example of the kind of default trust known as a resulting trust. The lender pays the money to the borrower by way of loan, but he does not part with the entire beneficial interest in the money, and insofar as he does not it is held on a resulting trust for the lender from the outset."

3. Absence of intention. If there is no intention to create a trust, title to the property may pass as an absolute gift to the donee: *Lassence v Tierney* (1848). Accordingly in *Lambe v Eames* (1871) the widow was able to keep the estate. If, however, the settlor had unsuccessfully declared himself to be a trustee, the property will remain in the settlor's estate. In *Re TXU Europe Group Plc (In Administration)* (2003) the issue was whether an investment portfolio (valued at more than £8 million) was held by a company on trust to provide top-up benefits to certain senior employees of the company. The High Court held that there was an absence of any positive indication of the intention to hold it on trust. Indeed, such indicators as there were pointed towards the opposite conclusion. For example, the company's accounts referred to the investment as an asset. It was also clear that the company's directors (the possible beneficiaries) did not, at the time of the investment, wish for a trust to be created because each would have incurred an immediate liability to tax. Accordingly, the money stayed with the company and was available to its general creditors.

Certainty of subject matter

The settlor must identify what is to be the subject of the trust and provide the means by which the interest of the beneficiaries can be ascertained. If not, the trust must fail because it cannot be enforced.

1. Trust property. The trust property, *i.e.* the subject matter of the trust, must be certain. Hence, there has to be an identifiable trust fund: *Hemmens v Wilson Browne* (1995). Accordingly, in *Palmer v Simmonds* (1854) a declaration concerning the "bulk of my estate" was held to be ineffective to create a trust. "Bulk" has no clear meaning and is totally uncertain. In *Re Goldcorp Exchange Ltd* (1995), a dealer in precious metals went into liquidation and a customer sought the delivery of gold that it had recently purchased. Unfortunately, the gold was unallocated and could not be individually identified. An implied trust, therefore, failed because of the uncertainty of its subject matter. In *Hunter v Moss* (1994), however, a trust of a specified number of shares in a company was upheld even though the particular shares were not identified. These two cases are difficult to reconcile. A distinction between these two cases is that one dealt with tangibles (gold) and the other with intangibles (shares). Also in *Goldcorp* the court was concerned with an implied trust whereas in *Hunter* the trust was express.

A trust of the residue of an estate may be valid. For example, if a testator leaves a will containing a number of legacies and creates a trust of "whatever is left" then there is certainty of subject matter. The executors could readily calculate the residual estate. There are cases, however, which appear to conflict and tend to confuse:

(i) in *the Estate of Last* (1958) property was left to a brother on terms that "at his death anything that is left, that came from me" was to pass to specified persons. This was held to be a trust because the brother only had a life interest in the property. Similarly, in *Re Thompson* (1879) the subject matter of the trust was identified as "should there be anything remaining" on a wife's death. This was upheld as a trust because the widow only had a life interest in her deceased husband's estate;

(ii) in *Sprange v Barnard* (1789), however, a wife left stock to her husband for his own use on terms that "the remaining part of what is left that he does not want for his own wants" should be bequeathed to specified individuals. The trust failed because there was a total uncertainty of subject matter. In *Re Jones* (1898), a trust of "such parts of my . . . estate as she shall not have sold" also failed for uncertainty of subject matter. In these two cases, the legatee was given an absolute interest in the property and, therefore, it could be entirely dissipated. Where, however, a life interest in the property is given, the capital cannot be touched and, therefore, the subject matter of the trust is known at the outset.

2. Beneficial interest. Except as regards discretionary trusts (see below), each beneficiary's share must be identified and allocated in some way: *Curtis v Rippon* (1820). For example, in *Boyce v Boyce* (1849), two houses were left on trust for two sisters, Maria and Charlotte. Maria was given the power to choose one house and Charlotte was to receive the other. Before making a choice Maria died. Although the subject matter of the trust was certain (*i.e.* the two houses), the trust failed because of uncertainty of beneficial interest. It was now impossible to say which house Charlotte should have. In *Re Golay* (1965), a trust was established to provide "a reasonable income for Tossy". Her beneficial interest was held to be certain because the use of the word "reasonable" provided an objective yardstick that the court could employ to calculate what a reasonable income for her would be. This provided the court with a method of ascertaining her beneficial interest. The court could look to her standard of living, income, needs, outgoings, etc. and conjure up an appropriate sum of money. This benevolent approach could not apply if the trust was of, say, "a reasonable legacy", "reasonable share", "reasonable amount" or "reasonable sum". The reasoning is that a reasonable income for an individual will be the same regardless of how much money is in the trust fund. It is capable of independent, objective assessment. Conversely, a reasonable share is subjective in that it may vary according to how much money is left. For example, if I use your lottery numbers and promise to give you a reasonable share of any eventual winnings then what is reasonable will vary wildly according to whether I win £10 or £10 million.

As regards *fixed* trusts, the equitable maxim "Equity is Equality" might be brought into play and save an otherwise invalid trust. This was demonstrated in *Burrough v Philcox* (1840) where a trust was set up to benefit the settlor's son and daughter. Their shares, however, were not specified. By relying upon the maxim, each was deemed to have an equal share. The maxim can be invoked only where there is no contrary intention shown. If the trust is "to benefit my children unequally", the maxim could not apply and the trust would necessarily fail. In relation to *discretionary* trusts, the very nature of such a trust entails that the beneficial interests are never certain. The essence of a discretionary trust is that the trustees exercise discretion as to who is to get what under the trust.

3. Uncertain subject matter.

(a) Where there is no certainty of trust property, there can be no trust. The property, whatever it is, will remain with the settlor or if he is dead will either pass by will or under the intestacy rules.

(b) If the trust fails for uncertainty of beneficial interest then, if the trust property has already been transferred to the trustee, it will be held on resulting trust for the settlor. If legal title has not moved, then the property remains with the settlor.

Certainty of objects

There have to be beneficiaries (*i.e.* the objects of the trust) who are certain or capable of being rendered certain: *Re Endacott* (1950). This is because there has to be someone who can enforce the trust. For example, in *Re TXU Europe Group Plc (In Administration)* (2003) it was unclear who the intended objects of the alleged trust were. Some evidence suggested that it was to benefit only existing executives and did not extend to future employees. Other evidence claimed that it was to benefit any employee whether past, present or future. Blackburne J. explained,

> "There is no reason, of course, why there should not be a trust for a class of persons which may increase in number. The evidence, however, must make this clear."

This rule does not, however, apply to charitable trusts because the Attorney General can enforce such public trusts. As will become clear, a private trust can fail for conceptual and evidential uncertainty, administrative unworkability or capriciousness. If a trust fails for a lack of certainty of objects, the property will (if it has left the settlor's estate) be held on resulting trust for the settlor.

1. Fixed trusts. In relation to fixed trusts (*i.e.* where the interests of the beneficiaries are specified in the trust instrument), the courts take a strict approach. The trust is void unless each and every beneficiary is ascertainable: *Morice v Bishop of Durham* (1804). This is called the "complete list" test. A trust will not fail, however, because a particular beneficiary cannot be found or there are doubts as to whether the beneficiary is still alive. In such cases, the money can be paid into court and steps then taken either to trace or to confirm the existence of the beneficiary. If the trustee decides eventually to distribute the trust property amongst the known beneficiaries, this will be done on the basis that any new claimant can recover against them: *Re Benjamin* (1902).

2. Discretionary trusts. A discretionary trust is where the trustee is given a discretion to select who, amongst a specified class of beneficiaries, will benefit under the trust. In modern times, the discretionary trust is used to benefit large groups of people such as employees and dependants. In such cases, a complete list might be a practical impossibility. Since *McPhail v Doulton* (1971), the rule for certainty of objects for discretionary trusts is the same as for powers of appointment. The test is whether it can be said with certainty of any potential claimant that he is or is not a member of the class.

In *McPhail v Doulton*, there was a trust to provide benefits for the staff of Matthew Hall & Co Ltd, their relatives and dependants. The trust deed stated that

> "The trustees shall apply the net income of the fund in making at their absolute discretion grants to or for the benefit of any of the officers and employees or ex-officers or ex-employees of the company or to any relatives or dependants of any such persons in such amounts at such times and on such conditions (if any) as they think fit".

The House of Lords held that it was no longer necessary to have a complete list in relation to discretionary trusts. The less strict "class test" was, instead, to be applied.

The issue remained as to whether the class test was to be rigidly applied, *i.e.* was it necessary to show of each and every claimant that they were or were not within a class? The potential problem lay with proving a negative: how can a trustee prove that a particular person is not, for example, a relative of the deceased? This issue was subsequently addressed in *Re Baden (No.2)* (1973). This case concerned a trust to benefit "relatives" and "dependants". Although the trust was upheld, the Court of Appeal did not speak with one voice concerning the class test:

(i) Megaw L.J. saw the test as being satisfied where, as regards a substantial number of beneficiaries, it can be said that they fall within the scope of the trust. This would be so even where there are others about whom it cannot be said with certainty whether they are in or outside the class. Accordingly, it did not matter that there were some "don't knows";

(ii) Stamp L.J. took the literal approach that the test could be satisfied only if it could be said of every potential claimant that they were or were not within the class. He explained:

"... validity or invalidity is to depend on whether you can say of any individual—and the accent must be on that word 'any' for it is not simply the individual whose claim you are considering who is spoken of—that he is or is not a member of the class for only thus can you make a survey of the range of objects or possible beneficiaries";

(iii) Sachs L.J. felt that the class test was that, if a potential claimant could not prove that he was within the class, he was presumed to be outside the class. Hence, there is no room for a "don't know" category.

3. Conceptual and evidential uncertainty. The description of the beneficiaries must, as regards both fixed and discretionary trusts, be conceptually certain. This refers to semantic or linguistic expression (*i.e.* precision of language) as regards the class that is to benefit. For example, in *Re Barlow* (1970) a trust to benefit "old friends" was conceptually uncertain. The terms "old" and "friend" have so many shades of meaning that it was impossible to say who was intended to benefit. As mentioned, in *Re Baden (No.2)*, the terms "relatives" and "dependants" were held to be conceptually certain. Evidential uncertainty is thought only to apply to fixed trusts (see Sachs L.J. in *Re Baden (No.2)*). Such uncertainty arises where there is an absence of evidence to show who was intended to benefit under the trust. For example, a fixed trust to benefit such students of Nutshell University who graduated in 1990 with a first class degree in law. If the records of Nutshell University have been destroyed by fire then it will be impossible to draw up a complete list of beneficiaries and, therefore, the trust will fail for evidential uncertainty.

4. Width of class and administrative unworkability. This is to do with the numbers of potential beneficiaries. In *McPhail v Doulton* (1971), Lord Wilberforce admitted that a class of beneficiaries might be so wide as not to constitute a class at all and this would make the trust (whether fixed or discretionary) administratively workable. By way of illustration, he suggested that a trust for "all the residents of Greater London" would be void. Hence, in *Re Hay's Settlement* (1982), it was accepted that a trust to benefit anyone in the world would be ineffective. In *R. v District Auditor Ex p. West Yorkshire Metropolitan County Council* (1986) an attempt to benefit "any or all the inhabitants in the County of West Yorkshire" failed because the class (approximately 2.5 million people) was too large. The courts are, however, not concerned with whether or not a power is administratively unworkable.

5. Capriciousness.   A trust can be void if it is capricious, *i.e.* it reflects a nonsensical intention on the part of the settlor and precludes any sensible consideration by the trustees. For example, a trust to benefit bald men would be struck down as capricious. In *Re Manisty's Settlement* (1974), Templeman J. provided the example of an attempt to benefit the residents of Greater London as being capricious. In *R. v District Auditor Ex p. West Yorkshire Metropolitan County Council*, however, the court held that the trust which purported to benefit 2.5 million inhabitants was not capricious. There have been no cases decided on the basis capriciousness. Similarly, a power can be rendered void if it is capricious.

Summary of rules on certainties

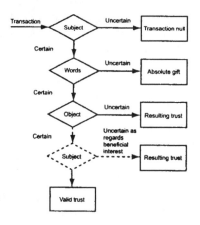

4. CONSTITUTION OF TRUSTS

Constitution relates simply to whether the trustee has legal title to the property. To be enforceable, a trust must be properly constituted. If not, there can be no trust. As Turner L.J. explained in *Milroy v Lord* (1862),

> " . . . the settlor must have done everything which according to the nature of the property comprised in the settlement was necessary to be done in order to render the settlement binding upon him . . . for there is no equity in this court to perfect an imperfect gift."

Milroy v Lord makes clear that there are two means by which a trust can be constituted:

(a) by transfer of legal title to trustee. The mechanism of transfer to be employed depends upon the nature of the property;

(b) by the settlor declaring himself as trustee.

Transfer to trustees

1. The settlor must transfer the title to the property to the trustee in the proper form.

(a) To transfer legal title to *land* a deed is needed (s.52 of the Law of Property Act 1925) and, in the case of registered land, this must generally be followed by the registration of the transfer at the Land Registry.

(b) Legal title to shares is transferred by an executed share transfer form followed by the name of the new owner being registered on the company's shareholding register: s.182(1) Companies Act 1985. Unlike a public company, a private company has a discretion to refuse to register a share transfer dealing. In such a case, legal title cannot pass.

(c) Title to chattels is transferred by physical delivery coupled with an intention to transfer. Delivery includes parting with dominion over an article (*e.g.* passing over the key to a jewellery box).

(d) Title to a cheque passes on the endorsement and delivery of the cheque to the third party. This is not possible, however, when the cheque is crossed "account payee only".

2. If the correct procedure is not followed, the transfer to the trustees will be ineffective. Examples of ineffective transfers include:

(a) *Richards v Delbridge* (1874) where Mr Delbridge purported to transfer title to a lease. He wrote on the back of the lease "this deed and all thereto belonging I give to Edward Burnetto Richards from this time forth with all the stock in trade". The gift failed because there was no deed specifically created to effect the transfer. It could not be argued that Mr Delbridge declared himself to be a trustee because he did not intend a trust to exist. He intended an outright gift.

(b) *Antrobus v Smith* (1806) where an endorsement on the back of a share certificate was ineffective to pass title to the shares. Similarly, in *Re Fry* (1946) a donor died after executing a share transfer, but (as he was resident abroad) he needed the consent of the Treasury to the transfer. He had not done this. Accordingly, the gift was ineffective.

3. If the donor has done everything he can do to transfer the gift but its effectiveness depends on some act of a third party, the gift will not fail. In *Re Rose* (1952), the donor executed a share transfer and handed it, together with the share certificate, to the donee. Although the transfer would not be complete until the shares had been registered by the company in the name of the donee, the gift was upheld. The donor had no more to do to perfect the gift. This is known as the "every effort doctrine". In *Re Fry* (1946), the problem was that the donor still had something to do himself and, therefore, had not made every effort.

4. There can be an effective assignment of an equitable interest without any need to transfer the legal estate to trustees: *Kekewich v Manning* (1851). This type of assignment has recently come to the fore in *Pennington v Waine* (2002), which concerned the legal title to 400 shares and, in particular, whether the shares had passed by way of gift. In 1998, Mr Pennington had a meeting with the donor, Ada, in which she said that she wanted to transfer immediately 400 shares in a company to her nephew, Harold. Ada signed an appropriate share transfer form and gave it to Mr Pennington. No further action was taken prior to Ada's death. Mr Pennington had, moreover, told Harold that no further steps had to be taken. Ada's will made no reference to the 400 shares. The issue that arose was whether the shares still formed part of Ada's residual estate.

Arden L.J. acknowledged that she had to determine what was necessary, in circumstances where the transaction was not for value, to effect a valid equitable assignment of shares. She concluded that the assignment was completed at the stage when it would be unconscionable for Ada to renege on the gift. As to whether it was necessary at law for Ada to deliver the form of transfer to Harold, it was held that this was not always a requirement of a valid equitable assignment and could, on the present facts, be dispensed with. As it would have been unconscionable for Ada to recall the gift, it followed that it would also be unconscionable for Ada's personal representative to refuse to hand over the share transfer to Harold after her death. Accordingly, there was a perfect gift of Ada's beneficial interest in the shares that took effect as a trust of the legal title in the shares.

Self-declaration of trust

1. A settlor with a legal or equitable interest can declare himself a trustee of the property for a beneficiary. He can do this orally, except in the case of land when the declaration must be evidenced in writing (s.53(1)(b) of the Law of Property Act 1925: see Ch.5). The settlor can use any form or words or his intention may be inferred from his conduct. In *Paul v Constance* (1977), Mr Constance received some compensation for an injury at work. Too embarrassed to open a joint account with his mistress, he opened it in his sole name. He did, however, intend that the money should be shared with her and, on more than one occasion, said to her that "this money is as much yours as mine". On his death Mrs Constance, his wife, claimed all the money. It was held that Mr Constance had declared a trust, albeit informally, of the account for himself and his mistress.

2. As mentioned, an ineffective gift will not be construed as a declaration of trust. This is because the settlor has shown his intention to give the property away absolutely. This is illustrated by the case of *Jones v Lock* (1865) where a father, who had failed to bring a gift home for his baby after working away, offered the child a cheque for £900 made out to the father. He passed it to the child saying "look you here. I give this to baby". The baby then began to tear up the cheque which was suitably removed from him and placed in a safe where it was found after the father's death. It was held to be an imperfect gift as the cheque had not been endorsed. The purported gift was evidence that the father did not intend to declare himself a trustee of the money.

In *Pennington v Waine* (2002), Arden L.J. acknowledged that, while an imperfect gift is not saved by being treated as a declaration of trust,

> " . . . where a court of equity is satisfied that the donor had an intention to make an immediate gift, the court will construe the words which the donor used as words effecting a gift or declaring a trust if they can fairly bear that meaning and otherwise the gift will fail."

Many commentators, however, think that the Court of Appeal here went too far and that its decision was based upon a misapplication of the earlier case of *T Choithram International v Pagarani* (2001).

In *T Choithram International v Pagarani* (2001), the settlor executed a deed of trust in favour of charitable organisation which he himself set up. He nominated himself and nine others as trustees. The settlor then purported orally to make an absolute gift of money and shares to the organization. He did not, however, transfer title of these assets to the other trustees. On his death, it was argued that the trust was incompletely constituted and that the assets would pass on intestacy to his next of kin. In the Privy Council, however, the trust was upheld. It was held that the settlor had done enough to declare himself a trustee. It did not matter that he intended to be one of a number of trustees (and not a sole trustee). In either case, it would be equally unconscionable for the settlor to renege on the declaration of trust.

Enforcement

A completely constituted trust is enforceable by all beneficiaries whether or not they have given consideration. An incompletely constituted trust can be enforced only by those beneficiaries who have given consideration. In this case "equity looks on as done that ought to be done". The imperfect transfer will then be treated as a contract to transfer which may be specifically enforced. If the beneficiaries have not given valuable consideration then they cannot enforce an incompletely constituted trust. Valuable consideration means money or money's worth or marriage. A settlement made before or in consideration of marriage, or one made in fulfillment of an ante-nuptial agreement, is made for value. Only certain people, however, are deemed to be within the marriage consideration. They are the husband, wife, children and, possibly, grandchildren. In *Re Plumptre's Marriage Settlement* (1910), the next-of-kin could not enforce a covenant to settle after-acquired property because they were volunteers. In *Pullan v Koe* (1913), however, children (being within marriage consideration) were able to enforce a similar covenant.

The principle that equity will not assist a volunteer may be sidestepped where there is unconscionability and by utilising the constructive trust. This was recognised in *Pennington v Waine* (2002) where, pending registration of the share transfer, the donor became the constructive trustee of the legal title to the shares for the donee.

After acquired (future) property

After acquired (or future) property is property that is not yet in existence. This could include, for example, expected royalties from a book or an anticipated inheritance under a will. This is to be contrasted with a vested or contingent future interest which has not yet fallen into possession. For example, "to A for life, remainder to C if he reaches 25 years of age". C's interest, although it may never vest, is already in existence and can be assigned.

In the absence of consideration, any assignment of property which might be acquired in the future is a nullity. In *Re Ellenborough* (1903), Lord Ellenborough's sister purported to convey, by a voluntary settlement, the property that she would receive under her brother's will. At that time, she had only a hope of obtaining the property. It was open for her brother to change his will. She could not be compelled to transfer the property. If, however, she had given consideration, equity would have enforced the voluntary settlement as a contract to convey the property when received.

Declarations of trust relating to future property are also void: *Williams v Commissioners of Inland Revenue* (1965). This rule gives way when consideration is given for, in such a case, equity will treat the declaration as a contract to create a trust.

Problems with covenants

Enforcement difficulties can arise where a settlor covenants to settle property on trust, but then changes his mind. There is no transfer at that stage so there is an incompletely constituted trust. There is merely a voluntary covenant in a deed, which is a gratuitous promise.

(a) In such a case, equity cannot interfere because it does not recognise the special character of a promise by deed and because it will not assist a volunteer. Hence, no equitable remedies will be available to the covenantee.

(b) The common law will, however, enforce a covenant. A party to the covenant can sue for breach in the normal way and recover full compensation: *Cannon v Hartley* (1949). The effect of the Contracts (Rights of Third Parties) Act 1999 should be noted as this allows third parties to sue even though they were not original parties to the covenant. The covenant must, however, expressly cater for third party enforcement or purport to confer a benefit on the third party. This would entail that, although not a party to the covenant, a purported beneficiary could be allowed to sue the covenantor directly. It is, however, possible to contract out of the 1999 Act.

(c) If the intended trustee is the only party (and the 1999 Act is contracted out of), the trustee might sue for breach. The beneficiary cannot because "equity does not assist a volunteer". The trustee's ability to sue is subject to major limitations. First, the intended trustee cannot be compelled by a beneficiary to sue the covenantor (*Re Pryce* (1917)). Indeed, a trustee ought not to pursue a remedy (*Re Kay's Settlement* (1939)). Secondly, there is doubt as to whether the trustee can recover full compensation. It is thought that only nominal compensation can be obtained (*Beswick v Beswick* (1968)). This is because the trustee has suffered no direct loss. Thirdly, even if the trustee recovers compensation, the damages would not be held on behalf of the beneficiaries. Instead, the money would be held on resulting trust for the covenantor/settlor (*i.e.* the person who the trustee has just sued!). It is thought that, under the rule in *Saunders v Vautier* (1841), the covenantor could discharge the resulting trust so as to prevent the intended trustee from embarking upon such pointless litigation.

(d) It is, however, possible that the covenantor might declare a trust of the covenant/promise itself. In *Fletcher v Fletcher* (1844), Ellis Fletcher covenanted with trustees to pay them

£60,000 to hold for his son, Jacob. He never gave the trustees the cash. Jacob succeeded in claiming the money by pleading that there was a completely constituted trust of the promise to pay the £60,000 and that he could enforce the trust of this promise. Accordingly, the subject matter of this trust was the covenant (*i.e.* the debt or chose in action) and not the money itself. This is a completely constituted trust of the benefit of the covenant and would be enforceable by a beneficiary who has not given consideration. There are, however, certain limitations on this type of trust:

(i) the intention to make a trust of the promise (and not a trust of what is promised) must be clearly demonstrated: *Vandepitte v Preferred Accident Assurance* (1933). In modern times, something like the following would be required: "the benefit of this covenant shall forthwith be held by my trustees upon trust";

(ii) it is debateable whether a trust of the covenant could cover after acquired property (*e.g.* shares acquired in the future). In *Re Cooks Settlement* (1965), the conclusion was that it could not embrace such future property. Nevertheless, there appears to be no good reason for this conclusion: see *Davenport v Bishopp* (1843).

To sum up, a covenant to transfer property is *prima facie* an improperly constituted trust. There has neither been an effective transfer to trustees nor a declaration of trust. It is, therefore, unenforceable by the beneficiary unless he has given consideration or is a party to the deed. In very limited cases, however, it may be possible to establish a completely constituted trust of the benefit of the covenant itself.

Exceptions: when equity will assist a volunteer

1. *Donationes mortis causa.* This category refers to a lifetime gift made in contemplation of death. The central notion of a DMC is that a gift by reason of death may, in certain circumstances, be perfected even though the necessary formalities of transfer have not been followed. Since *Sen v Headley* (1991), any type of property can, seemingly, be the subject of DMC: cheques, chattels, shares (even if in a private company), bonds, insurance policies, land, etc. The conditions for a valid DMC are that:

(a) the gift must have been made in contemplation of death: *Duffield v Elwes* (1827). Death must be thought by the donor to be imminent and there is required more than a general contemplation of death. In *Re Craven* (1937), it said that the contemplation must be of "death within the near future". Death must also be contemplated from a source (*e.g.* illness, subsequent to an accident, suicide, fear of a crash). This contemplation does not have to be expressed and can be inferred from the circumstances: *Walter v Hodge* (1818). The gift will still be perfected if the deceased dies from a different cause than was anticipated: *Wilkes v Arlington* (1931);

(b) the gift must be conditional on the death of the donor. As emphasised in *Cain v Moon* (1896), the gift must be made in circumstances that show that the property is to revert back to the donor if he recovers. As Nourse L.J. admitted in *Sen v Headley* (1991) the gift is absolute only on the donor's death, ". . . being revocable until that event occurs and ineffective if it does not." Accordingly, there can be no DMC if the donor intends to make an immediate gift. The condition can be express or inferred from the circumstances: *Gardner v Parker* (1818). The courts appear quite liberal on this point: see *Re Mustapha* (1891);

(c) control and possession must pass from the donor to the donee before death: *Ward v Turner* (1752). Words alone do not suffice for these purposes. There must, therefore, either be actual and physical delivery of an item or symbolic delivery by the passing over of indicia of title to the item (*e.g.* handing over title deeds to house: *Sen v Headley* (1991)). Hence, the passing of keys to a locked safe can pass dominion over its contents. In *Woodward v Woodward* (1995), the passing over of keys to a car sufficed to pass dominion over the vehicle. In *Re Weston* (1902), the passing over of a savings book constituted passing dominion of the savings themselves.

2. The rule in *Strong v Bird*. *Strong v Bird* (1874) concerned a scenario where a deceased creditor had appointed her debtor as an executor under a will. The facts involved the release of a £1000 debt and turned upon the presumed intention of the deceased. The rule simply put is that, where there is a purported gift (including the forgiveness of a debt) to a donee and the donee subsequently obtains legal title to the property in the capacity of a personal representative, the gift will then be perfected. The rule applies equally where the donee is appointed an administrator on the intestacy of the donor: *Re James* (1935).

This intention to forgive the debt has, however, to continue until death: see *Re Wale* (1956). In *Re Freeland* (1952), the promise to give a car at a future date fell outside the rule because there has to be an intention to make an immediate gift of the property. It should not, therefore, apply to a residuary gift (*i.e.* " the whatever is left" type of legacy).

In *Re Stewart* (1908), Neville J. explained the operation of the rule,

> "The reasoning is first that the vesting of the property in the executor at the time of the testator's death completes the imperfect gift made in the lifetime and secondly that the intention of the testator to give the beneficial interest to the executor is sufficient to countervail the equity of the beneficiaries under the will . . ."

3. Re Ralli's Will Trusts. A somewhat similar approach was adopted in *Re Ralli's Will Trusts* (1964) where a settlor entered into a covenant to transfer any existing or after acquired property to the trustee of her marriage settlement. No transfer was actually made to her trustee. On her death, title then vested in the executor who was fortuitously also a trustee under the marriage settlement. The fact that the trustee had title vested in him as executor perfected the otherwise imperfect trust. This differs from *Strong v* Bird in that *Re Ralli's Will Trusts* is not limited to executors/administrators and, moreover, there is no need for continuing intention on the part of the donor. As Parker & Mellows explain:

> " . . . if property of any type reaches without impropriety the hands of the person to whom it should already have been transferred as a trustee *inter vivos*, the trust in question will become completely constituted by transfer whether or not there is any continuing intention on the part of the settlor that this should occur".

It is to be appreciated, however, that *Ralli* has never been followed and doubts are raised as to whether it is good law.

4. Proprietary estoppel. An estoppel requires an assurance by one party (*e.g.* "the car is yours") and, on the faith of that assurance, detrimental reliance by the other party (*e.g.* by carrying out major repair works on the vehicle). In such circumstances the court may order the donor to complete the gift: *Pascoe v Turner* (1979). In *Dillwyn v Llewelyn* (1862), for example, a father assured his son that certain land now belonged to the son. The father did not, however, transfer the land to the son. The son then built a house on the land, but later the validity of the gift was challenged. The son was able to invoke estoppel and compel the gift to be perfected.

5. Conveyance of land to a minor. Although a minor cannot hold a legal estate in land, a purported conveyance to a minor is not totally ineffective. Under the Trusts of Land and Appointment of Trustees Act 1996, the conveyance will operate as a declaration that the land is held in trust for the minor. This is, therefore, a further (albeit statutory) exception to the rule that equity will not assist a volunteer.

5. FORMALITIES

In order to be effective some types of trust must adhere to a prescribed form. The most usual insistence is that the transaction either be in writing or be evidenced (recorded) in writing.

Why formalities?

Formalities are imposed primarily in order to protect the parties when property is held on trust. More specifically, the formality requirements are designed to:

   (i) provide documentary evidence in order to minimise fraud;
  (ii) provide a provable record of transactions;
 (iii) instil certainty as to what the parties intended;
 (iv) establish the obligations of the trustee;
  (v) deter secret transactions; and
 (vi) raise revenue for the Treasury by way of stamp duty.

Trusts of personalty

No extra formalities are required in relation to an *inter vivos* trust of personalty (*i.e.* not a trust of land): see *Paul v Constance* (1977).

Trusts created by will

All testamentary trusts must comply with s.9 of the Wills Act 1837 (as amended). This provides that:

"No will shall be valid unless:
(a) it is in writing, and signed by the testator or by some other person in his presence and by his direction; and
(b) it appears that the testator intended by his signature to give effect to the will; and
(c) the signature is made or acknowledged by the testator in the presence of two or more witnesses present at the same time; and
(d) each witness either:
  (i) attests and signs the will; or
  (ii) acknowledges his signature in the presence of the testator (but not necessarily in the presence of any other witness)".

Trusts of land

Section 53(1)(b) of the Law of Property Act 1925 provides that:

"a declaration of trust respecting any land or any interest therein must be manifested and proved by some writing signed by some person who is able to declare such a trust or by his will".

Due to the value of land, and the highly technical rules that attend its transfer, it is traditionally treated differently than other types of property. Hence, the extra formalities of s.53(1)(b) are justified.

Section 53(1)(b) does not require that the trust be declared in writing, but does demand that a trust of land be evidenced in writing. The writing (which can be a will) can come into existence after the trust has been declared, but must contain all the terms of the trust: *Smith v Matthew* (1861). There is no prescribed form for this writing to take and it can span more than one document. The signature of the settlor is, however, required. There is no express mention made here of the ability of an agent to sign the document. The absence of writing does not make the trust void, but instead makes it unenforceable by a beneficiary.

The section does not, however, apply to resulting, implied or constructive trusts (s.53(2)). Sometimes the court will imply a constructive trust from the facts in order to take an otherwise unenforceable outside the ambit of the formalities. This occurred in *Rouchefoucald v Bousted* (1897) where there was a purely oral trust of land that was, at face value, unenforceable. As the claimant had acted to his detriment on the strength of this otherwise enforceable trust, the court felt that not to enforce the trust would amount to a fraud. The court, therefore, implied a constructive trust and sidestepped the need for formalities. A similar stance was adopted in both *Bannister v Bannister* (1948) and *Hodgson v Marks* (1971).

Dealing with an existing trust interest

Section 53(1)(c) of the Law of Property Act 1925 provides that

> "a disposition of an equitable interest or trust subsisting at the time of the disposition, must be in writing signed by the person disposing of the same or by his agent thereunto lawfully authorised in writing or by will".

It is crucial to appreciate that s.53(1)(c) applies only after a trust has been created. It has no relevance to the actual declaration of the trust under which the equitable interest arises. Put in other terms, this means that s.53(1)(c) can apply only where the legal and equitable interests in the property have already been fragmented. Accordingly, it is designed to operate on an assignment of an equitable interest by a beneficiary to someone else or where the beneficiary directs the trustee to hold the trust property on behalf of another.

The disposition (*i.e.* transfer) of the equitable interest has itself to be made in writing and not merely be supported by documentary evidence (*cf.* s.53(1)(b)). There is no scope here for the subsequent ratification in writing. Note that the signature of an agent is expressly permitted by s.53(1)(c). An absence of writing makes the transfer void. The section applies to all property: personal property as well as land.

Not all dealings with an equitable interest are, however, caught by s.53(1)(c).

(a) The disclaimer of an equitable interest by a beneficiary does not amount to an assignment. In *Re Paradise Motor Co Ltd* (1968), a stepfather gave an equitable interest in some shares to his stepson. When the stepson discovered this, he made it clear he did not want them. Subsequently he changed his mind. His argument that the disclaimer was ineffective because it was not in writing to comply with s.53(1)(c) was rejected.

(b) In circumstances where an equitable owner declares a trust of his own interest, whether s.53(1)(c) applies turns upon whether or not the equitable owner has active duties to perform. By way of illustration, A is the trustee and B is the beneficiary. If B then declares a discretionary trust in favour of C and D, it will fall outside s.53(1)(c). It will be treated as a valid *declaration* of trust. If, however, B simply declares a fixed trust for C and D, and has no active duties to perform, he will be regarded as having assigned his equitable interest in which case the transaction will be invalid unless it satisfies the requirements of s.53(1)(c). Assuming the assignment is valid, B will drop out of the picture and A will hold directly for C and D: *Grainge v Wilberforce* (1889).

(c) Where an assignee of an equitable interest is to hold in a fiduciary capacity, there is no need for the writing to contain all the terms of the trust *(cf.* a declaration of trust of land which must do so by virtue of s.53(1)(b)). In *Re Tyler* (1967), Miss Tyler appointed King and Green executors under her will. Shortly afterwards, she gave £1,500 to King. Subsequently, she wrote to King instructing him to use the money for Green as she had previously directed. After she had paid the money to King, there was a resulting trust in her own favour. Although the letter did not contain every detail of the assignment, the letter amounted to a valid assignment of that equitable interest.

(d) In *Neville v Wilson* (1996), an oral agreement, that had the effect of making each shareholder a constructive trustee for the others, was upheld. Similarly, in *Gold v Hill* (1998), an oral direction by the holder of the life policy to the nominated beneficiary of the policy that, in the event of the policyholder's death, the beneficiary should hold the policy for the benefit of the deceased's family was not regarded as an assignment of the equitable interest. The direction operated like a secret trust in that nothing was transferred until the death of the policyholder.

(e) The provision does not apply to resulting, implied or constructive trusts (s.53(2)).

Section 53(1)(c): the key cases

Sometimes it is not clear whether a transaction amounts to the declaration of trust or is, instead, the disposition of an equitable interest. The cases appear inconsistent and illogical. This is because many of them are tax avoidance cases that involve the Inland Revenue. As dispositions have to be in writing and writing attracts stamp duty, the Inland Revenue tends to argue for a disposition rather than a declaration. Stamp duty is charged on an instrument rather than on the transaction itself. In *Bishop Square Ltd v Inland Revenue Commissioners* (1997), for example, the Inland Revenue sought stamp duty of £372,230 whereas the taxpayer claimed that the duty was a mere 50p. The outcome (which favoured the Inland Revenue) turned upon an oral transfer being invalid under s.53(1)(c). Similarly, in the *Vandervell* cases (see below), it was in the interest of the Inland Revenue to establish, for tax reasons, that an oral disposition had been ineffective due to a lack of writing. The following principles arise from the cases.

(a) On an assignment of an equitable interest, two documents can be read together: *Re Danish Bacon Co Ltd Staff Pension Fund Trust* (1971). In that case, an employee nominated his wife to receive benefits under a pension scheme should he die before he was entitled. He signed the approved form. Later he changed the nominated beneficiary by a letter. Although doubtful as to whether the nomination was an assignment of a subsisting equitable interest within s.53(1)(c), Megarry J. held that, even if it was, the two documents could together constitute the necessary writing.

(b) A direction to trustees to hold on trust for another comes within s.53(1)(c) and so must be in writing. In *Grey v Inland Revenue Commissioners* (1960), a settlor made six settlements of nominal sums in favour of his grandchildren. Subsequently he transferred shares to trustees to hold on a bare trust for himself. He then orally directed the trustees to hold those shares on the trusts of the grandchildren's settlements. The settlor, thereby, attempted to do everything orally so as to escape stamp duty. The trustees then executed documents confirming they held the shares on the trusts of the settlements. The House of Lords held that the written confirmation of the new trusts by the trustees was, in effect, a disposition within s.53(1)(c) by the beneficiary under the bare trust. This transferred the equitable interest to the beneficiaries of the settlements. Thus the oral direction was ineffective. The documents executed by the trustees were not merely confirmatory. Instead they operated to effect the disposition and stamp duty was payable on those documents.

(c) An oral direction by a beneficiary to trustees holding on a bare trust for him to transfer the legal as well as the equitable interest to a third party will be effective. The formal transfer of the legal ownership will automatically carry with it the equitable interest without a separate written disposition of that interest. In *Vandervell v Inland Revenue Commissioners* (1967), the National Provincial Bank was holding shares on a bare trust for Mr. Vandervell. He directed the Bank to transfer the shares to the Royal College of Surgeons subject to an option to repurchase for £5,000 that was given to the Vandervell trustees. An argument by the Inland Revenue that he needed a document to transfer the equitable interest in the shares failed. It was crucial that the legal and equitable title to the shares moved within the same transaction. As Lord Upjohn explained:

"Where the beneficial owner owns the whole beneficial estate and is in a position to give directions to his bare trustee with regard to the legal as well as the equitable estate there can be no possible ground for invoking the section where the beneficial owner wants to deal with the legal estate as well as the equitable estate".

It is, however, important that legal and equitable ownership vested in one body (the Royal College of Surgeons). The outcome might have been much different if Mr. Vandervell had not dealt with the legal title at all or, indeed, had attempted to move legal title one way and equitable title another.

The Inland Revenue, however, succeeded in establishing that Mr. Vandervell had not divested himself of the equitable interest in the option to repurchase the shares. Although the legal title to the option was validly vested in the Vandervell trustees, no mention had been made of the equitable title. Accordingly, as the terms of the trusts had not been spelt out, there was a resulting trust to Mr.

Vandervell of the benefit of the option. Mr. Vandervell
was, therefore, liable to pay tax. As Lord Wilberforce
pointed out, an equitable interest cannot exist in the
abstract and must be vested somewhere.

(d) To continue with the Vandervell saga, in 1961 Mr.
Vandervell instructed his trustees to exercise the option
given to them. The trustees used £5,000 from a trust for
Mr. Vandervell's children. The Inland Revenue claimed
that Mr. Vandervell had not disposed of his equitable
interest in the shares. In 1965, Mr. Vandervell executed a
document by which he transferred any interest he had in
the shares to his trustees to hold on trust for his children.
The shares were then worth around £1 million. Mr.
Vandervell then died and his executors claimed that his
estate, and not his children, was beneficially entitled to
the shares. The executors based this claim upon the fact
that there had been no written transfer of the equitable
interest.

The dispute reached the Court of Appeal and is known as
Re Vandervell Trusts (No.2) (1973). The court held that
there had been a valid declaration of trust by the trustees
in 1961 when they exercised the option. This declaration
had the effect of terminating the resulting trust in favour
of Mr. Vandervell. The estate was not, therefore, entitled
to the shares. As Lord Denning explained,

> "A resulting trust for the settlor is born and dies without
> writing at all. It comes into existence whenever there is a gap
> in the beneficial ownership. It ceases to exist whenever that
> gap is filled by someone becoming beneficially entitled. As
> soon as the gap is filled by the creation or declaration of a
> valid trust, the resulting trust comes to an end".

This case has been heavily criticised. It is difficult on the
facts to find that there was a genuine declaration of trust.
It is also difficult to understand why, as there was a
resulting trust of the option, there was not also a resulting
trust of the shares that resulted from the exercise of such
option. The practical consequence was that the beneficial
interest passed from Mr. Vandervell to his children under
their settlements. This, however, seems very much like a
disposition. Perhaps a clue is to be found from Lord
Denning's admission that, " . . . hard cases make bad law,
but we want justice". The Court of Appeal felt that it

would be unfair on both Mr. Vandervell and his children not to uphold the trust.

(e) A formal transfer of shares following an oral agreement amounts to an assignment for the purposes of s.53(1)(c). In *Oughtred v Inland Revenue Commissioners* (1960), the trustees held shares for the benefit of Mrs. Oughtred for life with remainder to her son, Peter. In return for some shares of his mother's, Peter made an oral contract to transfer his interest in remainder to her. Subsequently, formal transfers were executed transferring these shares to the mother. The Inland Revenue claimed stamp duty on the transfers as they were the documents that effectively transferred the interest.

The mother contended that, by virtue of the doctrine of conversion that operates on a specifically enforceable contract, the equitable interest had already passed to her. Hence, the writing transferred nothing. The majority of the House of Lords rejected this line of reasoning. The contract did not pass the full equitable interest in the shares and, therefore, the document was subject to stamp duty. This appears to be a sensible conclusion as, if the contract was rescinded or specific performance ceased to be available, the entire equitable interest would remain with the son.

6. SECRET TRUSTS

It was in order to prevent s.9 of the Wills Act 1837 being used as an instrument of fraud that the doctrine of secret trusts was developed. The problem with a secret trust is that it may not appear on the face of the will (*i.e.* a fully secret trust) or, if mention is made of its existence, its terms will not be disclosed (*i.e.* a half secret trust).

A secret trust involves the testator leaving a legacy to a trusted person (*e.g.* a solicitor) who has been told in confidence how to apply the funds. The legacy may either appear to be absolute (as with a fully secret trust) or disclose the trust without revealing its object (as with a half secret trust). Of course, problems will arise if this trusted friend fails to carry out the undertaking. It is then necessary to consider whether the court can compel the performance of the trust.

The traditional purpose of a secret trust is to keep the identity of the beneficiary undisclosed (*e.g.* the secret beneficiary is the testator's illegitimate child or mistress). This might be viewed as necessary because, once probate is granted, a will becomes a document of public record. It can be inspected by anyone who pays the appropriate fee. A further reason for using a secret trust is to allow changes and future dispositions to be made without adherence to the Wills Act. A fully secret trust also affords flexibility for a testator who cannot quite make up his mind what to leave to whom. His instruction to his trustee might change several times before his death. As will become clear, the same flexibility does not, however, apply to half secret trusts.

Justification for secret trusts

It is apparent that secret trusts form an exception to the formalities imposed by the Wills Act, but the decided cases give little thought to why secret trusts are treated differently. There has to be some justification for equity to override a statutory provision in this way. There are three schools of thought as to what is the underlying rationale for the law relating to secret trusts. Unfortunately, none of them is entirely satisfactory.

1. *Dehors* the will.   The modern (and best) view is that a fully secret or half secret trust operates *"dehors"* (outside) the will: *Re Young* (1951). In other words, the trust arises not from the will, but from its lifetime communication to and acceptance by the trustee. Hence, the theory is that the rules governing wills should not apply to secret trusts. Instead, they are enforceable because of the personal obligations placed on the trustee. In *Re Young* (1951), the testator made a bequest to his wife with a direction that on her death she should leave the property for the purposes he had already communicated to her. One of these purposes was that she should give the chauffeur £2,000. Although the chauffeur had witnessed the will, he was entitled to the money. He did not forfeit his legacy under s.15 of the Wills Act that prevents a witness to a will being a beneficiary under it.

The *dehors* theory means that the communication to the trustee is an *inter vivos* declaration of a trust to which the Wills

Act has no application. The vesting of the property in the secret trustees by the will constitutes the trust. If the trust property is land, however, s.53(1)(b) creates a potential problem as the trust as to be evidenced in writing. If the communication of trust was made in letter form and signed by the testator, then all is well. If the communication was oral, a constructive trust would have to be implied to take advantage of s.53(2) which states that the formalities do not apply to such trusts.

2. Incorporation by reference. It is sometimes suggested that the requirement that communication and acceptance of a half secret trust take place before the will is made, and the rule that the will must not contradict what actually happened, result from a confusion with the doctrine of incorporation by reference. This is a doctrine of probate law and allows incorporation of a written document into the will when the will specifically refers to it. For example, the will might state "I devise Blackacre to X on the trusts which I have communicated to him by a letter dated May 2, 2004". This letter is then admitted to probate together with the will.

The element of secrecy is lost when documents are incorporated. The result of the doctrine is that it is as if the document was contained in the will itself (*i.e.* it becomes a public document).

Unlike a trustee in a half secret trust, a trustee by incorporation need not know about the document until the testator dies. A beneficiary under the document will, however, lose the gift if he witnesses the will.

Although some judges have believed incorporation to be the basis of secret trusts, it is now a largely discredited theory. The difficulties with it are that secret trusts need not be declared in a document (they can be oral), the trust entirely loses its secrecy and it would need to be communicated to the trustee before the will is executed.

3. Fraud. The nineteenth century view was that secret trusts were enforced to prevent fraud. This is an outmoded view and often criticized.

In relation to a fully secret trust, the theory is that it would be a fraud for the legatee to keep the legacy for himself. As a statute cannot be used an as instrument of fraud, the secret trust can be enforced even though the otherwise necessary formalities are absent. As the secret beneficiary is a volunteer, a resulting trust should usually arise and the money revert back to the estate. It is odd that, instead, the benefit "projects forward" to the secret beneficiary.

A further problem with this approach is that, as regards a half secret trust, the fraud is not so obvious. The trust is declared on the face of the will and there is no way that the legatee can keep the legacy. It is a weak argument to suggest that it amounts to a fraud on the secret beneficiary. This would allow any trust to be enforced regardless of a disregard of the required formalities.

Fully secret trusts

(a) As mentioned, it appears from the will that the legatee is entitled to take the legacy absolutely. No indication of a trust is discernible from the will itself. For example, a legacy of "£50,000 for Fred". If Fred had previously agreed to the testator's request that he would hold it on trust for Mavis, Fred will not be able to keep the money. Instead, a fully secret trust will exist and Fred will be compelled to carry out the trust. It is also possible that a fully secret trust could arise on intestacy (where no will exists). If an owner of property does not make a will because X (the person entitled on intestacy) has agreed to hold it for a secret beneficiary, then the trust is seemingly enforceable against X: *Re Gardner* (1920). In *Ottaway v Norman* (1972), the testator agreed with his housekeeper that she could have his bungalow after his death provided that she, in turn, left it to the testator's son and daughter-in-law on her own death. She agreed to this and the testator left the bungalow to her absolutely. On her death, however, she left the property to another. The court held the son and daughter-in-law were entitled to the property.

(b) The essential element in a secret trust is that the obligation to hold the property on trust must have been communicated and accepted by the trustee prior to the testator's death. It is, however, not necessary that the communication of the trust occur before the will is drafted (*cf.* a half secret trust). In *Wallgrave v Tebbs* (1855), the testator left money in his will to Tebbs and Martin. After the testator's death, a draft letter was found specifying how the testator wanted them to hold the money. The court held that, because there had been no communication of this to Tebbs and Martin before the testator's death, there could be no binding trust. Tebbs and Martin could, therefore, take the money.

(c) The testator must impose a legal (and not merely moral) obligation on his secret trustee. In *McCormick v Grogan* (1869), the testator sent a weakly worded letter to the intended trustee stating,

> "I do not wish you to act strictly to the foregoing instructions, but leave it entirely to your own good judgment to do as you think I would do if living and as the parties are deserving".

The House of Lords concluded that there was no secret trust as no binding obligation was put on the legatee. The legatee could keep the money for himself. A similar approach was adopted in *Re Snowden* (1979) where the legatee again accepted only a moral obligation.

(d) There must be acceptance by the trustee of the legal obligation to hold the property on secret trust. This acceptance can be express or implied by acquiescence and silence (*Wallgrave v Tebbs* (1855); *Ottaway v Norman* (1972)). Of course, this entails that the legatee can expressly reject the role of trustee and, in doing so, keep any legacy under the will.

(e) There are potential difficulties if the gift is to two legatees and only one has accepted the trust. In *Re Stead* (1901), Farwell J. laid down somewhat elaborate rules that hinged upon whether the legatees were *joint tenants* or *tenants in common*. If the former, both would hold on trust; if the latter, the trust would bind only the party that undertook the obligation. As regards half secret trusts, the trustees always hold as joint tenants. A simpler view is to consider whether the legacy has been induced by a promise, albeit made only by one of them, that the property would be held on the terms of a secret trust. If so both legatees should be bound.

(f) The terms of the trust (*e.g.* the subject matter of the trust and the beneficiaries) must be communicated to the trustee before the testator's death. Communication can be oral or by letter. If not, the trust will fail. In such a case, provided that the testator had informed the legatee of the intention to create a trust, it will not be possible for the legatee to lay claim to the money: *Re Boyes* (1884). The money will, instead, remain in the testator's estate. It is possible, however, that communication of the terms of the trust can be implied. The classic example is where the trustee is given a letter marked "not to be opened until after my death". Provided this is handed to the secret trustee in the testator's lifetime, it will amount to constructive communication of the terms of the trust: *Re Keen* (1937). The court likened the trustee's position to a ship sailing under sealed orders.

(g) Any addition to the trust fund must also be communicated to the trustees. In *Re Colin Cooper* (1939) a testator left £5,000 to trustees on the terms that he had communicated to them. Without telling them, however, he increased the sum to £10,000 by codicil. It was held that they held the initial £5,000 on the terms of the trust, but that the remaining £5,000 went back to the estate by way of resulting trust. As regards the latter sum, there had simply been no communication and acceptance.

Half secret trusts

(a) A half secret trust arises where, on the face of the will, property is given to X as trustee, but the terms of the trust are not disclosed. For example, "£50,000 to X on trust for the purposes I have communicated to him". X, of course, cannot take the property beneficially so there is not the same risk of fraud as with a fully secret trust. Nevertheless, as the trustee has undertaken a binding obligation, he will be compelled to perform the terms of the trust.

(b) There can sometimes be difficulties in classifying whether a trust is fully secret or half secret. For example, "£50,000 to X knowing that he will carry out my wishes as I have communicated to him". The problem is that the testator has used precatory words (see Ch.3) that no longer import a trust. Accordingly, this should create a fully secret trust and not, as it may first appear, a half secret trust: *Irvine v Sullivan* (1869). There the wording of the will was "trusting that she will carry out my wishes with regard to the same, with which she is fully acquainted". This amounted to a fully secret trust.

(c) The testator must communicate that a trust is intended either before or, at the latest, contemporaneously with the execution of the will: *Blackwell v Blackwell* (1929). If there is no communication or late communication, a resulting trust will arise in favour of the deceased's estate. The trustee cannot keep the legacy because the will makes it clear that this was not intended: *Re Boyes* (1884).

(d) The terms of the trust must be sufficiently communicated to the trustee. It is sufficient if he is handed an envelope marked "not to be opened before my death", but he must know that in the envelope are the terms of the secret trust: *Re Keen* (1937). In that case, however, the half secret trust failed. The testator left property in his will "upon such trusts as may be notified by me to them (*i.e.* his executors and trustees) during my lifetime". A sealed envelope was given to the trustees, but the trust failed because it referred to future communications and fell foul of principle laid down in *Blackwell v Blackwell* (1929).

Distinctions to be drawn: a summary

(a) As already mentioned, communication and acceptance in a fully secret trust can be at any time before the testator dies. As regards a half secret trust, communication and acceptance must be before or at the same time as the execution of the will.

(b) In a fully secret trust it does not matter that the will contradicts the trust. The fact that the trustee appears in the will to take beneficially is itself a contradiction, but to allow the trust to fail on that count would be to undermine the whole basis of secret trusts. In a half secret trust there can be no conflict between the will and the trust.

(c) Under s.15 of the Wills Act 1837, a beneficiary who witnesses a will loses his interest. In a fully secret trust, the trustee appears in the will as an absolute legatee. If the secret trustee has witnessed the will, therefore, it is thought that no property can vest in the trustee. Accordingly, the trust for the secret beneficiaries is never constituted. Hence, the fully secret trust should fail. In a half secret trust, however, the problem does not arise because the will makes clear that the trustee cannot take beneficially in any event. Accordingly, it does not matter if either the trustee or the secret beneficiary witnesses the will.

(d) If the trustee predeceases the testator in a fully secret trust, the trust should fail. There is a failure of the legacy on which the trust was to operate: *Re Maddock* (1902). As regards a half secret trust where there a trust is evident from the will, equity will not allow the trust to fail for want of a trustee: *Re Armitage* (1972).

7.　THE STATUTORY AVOIDANCE OF TRUSTS

The general rule is that once a trust has been completely constituted it cannot be revoked by the settlor. Real ownership has become vested in the beneficiaries. At common law, this rule gives way where:

(a) there is an express power of revocation in the settlement;

(b) the settlor was induced to make the settlement by fraud or undue influence or it was made under some fundamental mistake or misapprehension as to its nature or effect;

(c) the trust is merely only an arrangement for the more convenient payment of creditors. This is sometimes called an "illusory trust" (*i.e.* it is not a real trust). This type of trust can be revoked unless the creditors have executed the trust instrument; relied to their detriment upon it or the trust is to take effect only on the settlor's death; or

(d) the trust is unlawful (sometimes called an "illegal trust") by reason of contravening morality or public policy, the provisions of a statute or the law of perpetuities. The latter concerns, for example, the vesting of property at too remote a time in the future.

Parliament has, however, introduced more sweeping powers whereby the court can set aside a gift or transfer to a trustee. Put broadly, these powers arise in the context of transactions to put property unfairly beyond the reach of creditors, spouses and family.

Transactions defrauding creditors

There is often a conflict between the claims of a settlor's family and his creditors. As will be shown in Ch.8, there are permitted ways of protecting property under protective trusts. Although the law strives to let a man do what he wants with his own property, a trust created by a settlor with the intention of defeating his creditors can be set aside under the Insolvency Act 1986.

Sections 423–425 of the 1986 Act give the court a power to prevent a trust being used unfairly to disadvantage creditors. This power arises when the court is satisfied that a transaction was entered into at an undervalue for the purpose of putting assets beyond the reach of the creditor or otherwise prejudicing his interests. For these purposes "undervalue" includes:

(i) making a gift;
(ii) entering into a transaction without consideration;
(iii) entering into a transaction in consideration of marriage; and
(iv) accepting a consideration that does not reflect the true value of the property.

The interests of certain classes are, however, shielded against the effect of an order under the 1986 Act. These include third parties that acquire property (or a benefit from the transaction) in good faith and for value without notice of the circumstances which gave rise to the order. In *Agricultural Mortgage Corp v Woodward* (1995), a farmer's land was mortgaged to the AMC. He granted a tenancy to his wife so that the mortgagee would not be able to sell the land with vacant possession. Although the wife paid a full market rent, this was treated as a transaction at an undervalue and was set aside. The real benefit acquired by the wife was much greater than the rent she paid because she was in a position to demand a ransom for surrendering her tenancy so as to make the farm available to the creditor.

The court must be satisfied that the person who enters into a transaction at an undervalue has the intention of prejudicing a creditor. Dishonesty is not essential and the transaction may have been made on the strength of legal advice. In *Moon v Franklin* (1990), the necessary intention was shown where a husband, threatened with legal proceedings, made substantial gifts to his wife from the proceeds of the sale of his business.

Insolvency

Sections 339–342 of the Insolvency Act 1986 give the court wide powers to set aside, on the application of the trustee in bankruptcy, settlements where an individual is adjudged bankrupt and has previously entered into transactions at an undervalue or given a preference to another.

1. Undervalue. "Undervalue" is given the same definition as considered above. There will, however, be a rebuttable presumption of undervalue where the transaction was entered into with an associate. An associate is exhaustively defined in s.435 and includes spouses, relatives, partners and employers. Certain time limits are, moreover, imposed in relation to undervalue transactions by a bankrupt:

(i) *two years.* If a bankruptcy petition is presented within two years of any such transaction then an order can be made in respect of it notwithstanding that the individual was solvent at the time;

(ii) *five years.* If a bankruptcy petition is presented within five years of any such transaction then an order can be made in respect of it unless the individual can prove that he was solvent at the time without the property included in the transaction.

2. Preference. A "preference" occurs where a debtor puts one of his creditors in a better position than the creditor would have otherwise been in should the debtor's bankruptcy ensue. The court can only make an order where the individual was "influenced in deciding to give" the preference "by a desire to produce" this result. This will be presumed, unless the contrary is shown, where preference is given to an associate. Certain time limits operate in relation to a preference:

(i) *six months.* The court can make an order concerning a preference given in the six months preceding the bankruptcy petition unless the individual was solvent at the time without the property included in the preference;

(ii) *two years.* Where the preference is given to an associate, the court can make an order relating to a preference given in the two years preceding the bankruptcy petition unless the individual was (discounting the property included in the preference) solvent at the time.

3. Definition. For these purposes, "insolvency" is defined in s.341 of the 1986 Act. This provides that an individual (who enters into a transaction at an undervalue or gives a preference) is insolvent if:

(i) he is unable to pay his debts as they fall due; or

(ii) the value of his assets is less than the amount of his liabilities, taking into account his possible and prospective liabilities.

4. Protection of third parties. Protection is offered to third parties that acquire property from someone other than the debtor. This protection is dependent upon the third party having acted in good faith and having given value. On fulfilling these conditions, a person who acquires a benefit from a transaction will not have to pay any sums to the trustee in bankruptcy.

Special provision is made in relation to land. The Insolvency (No.2) Act 1994 protects a purchaser of land in circumstances where a gift or transaction at an undervalue appears on the title and the time limits for setting it aside have not expired. He will not be protected, however, where:

(i) he had notice of the transaction at an undervalue or the preference given and that the earlier transferor had been adjudged bankrupt or that a petition had been presented; or

(ii) he was an associate or connected with the bankrupt or the person with whom the bankrupt entered into the transaction or gave a preference.

Marital breakdown

Section 37 of the Matrimonial Causes Act 1973 allows transactions to be set aside on the breakdown of a marriage. This can occur where the court is satisfied that one spouse is about to make a disposition with the intention of depriving the other of financial relief under the Act. In such a case, the court can set aside a disposition already made unless it was made for valuable consideration to a bona fide purchaser without notice of any intention to defeat the applicant's claim.

Family claims

Under s.10 of the Inheritance (Provision for Family and Dependants) Act 1975, the court has a discretionary power to make provision for spouses and dependants. This caters for the situation where they have not been adequately provided for under the deceased's will or according to the rules of intestacy. In order to defeat such an attempt to claim his estate, the deceased might attempt to give away his property. Section 10 provides that donees of such gifts that were made within six years prior to the death of the donor can be ordered to provide sums of money (or other property not exceeding the value of the gift) in order that financial provision can be made.

---

8. PROTECTIVE TRUSTS

In the previous chapter, it was demonstrated that a trust, which is designed to sidestep the Insolvency Act 1986, is liable to be set aside. This chapter, however, considers certain indirect means that may allow a settlor to achieve a similar goal.

A protective trust is employed when the settlor wishes to protect property against an improvident beneficiary and/or the claims of his creditors. Traditionally, the means by which this can be achieved are somewhat elaborate. The settlor will give the beneficiary what is known as a "determinable life interest" which upon "forfeiture" is succeeded by a "discretionary trust" for a class of beneficiaries (of which the original beneficiary may be one).

Following the Trustee Act 1925, the process of creating a protective trust has been greatly simplified. It was once necessary to set out the terms of the protective trust in detail. Since 1925, however, all the settlement must now do is contain reference to the intention to create a protective trust. The terms of that trust are then implied by s.33. This section provides that the income will be held upon trust for the principal beneficiary until his protected life interest is forfeited. On the failure of this life interest, the income is to be held upon discretionary trust for the benefit of:

(a) the principal beneficiary, his spouse and children; or
(b) if there is no spouse or children, the principal beneficiary and the persons who would, if he were actually dead, be entitled to the trust property.

Determinable life interests

It is sometimes difficult to distinguish between "conditional interests" and "determinable interests". A *determinable interest* is a limited interest where the limit is set at the outset. A *conditional interest* is a full interest that is liable to be cut short by a condition subsequent. Hence, the interest may never run its full course.

In practice, the easiest way of distinguishing between these two legal concepts lies in the words used. Words and expressions such as "while," "during," "as long as" and "until" indicate a determinable interest. Expressions such as "on condition that" and "provided that" indicate a conditional interest. The importance of the distinction is that the court does not favour conditional interests. A gift to a beneficiary provided that (or on condition that) he does not become bankrupt is, therefore, void.

In contrast, a gift to a beneficiary until he becomes bankrupt is perfectly valid. This is not so, however, where it is the settlor's own bankruptcy that the settlor is attempting to guard against. In *Re Burroughs-Fowler* (1916), an ante-nuptial settlement placed property on trust to pay the income to the settlor for life or until certain events should happen, one of which was his bankruptcy. He went bankrupt whereupon his trustee in bankruptcy became entitled to his life interest.

The settlor can, however, protect himself against events other than bankruptcy. In *Re Detmold* (1889), there was a marriage settlement of the settlor's own property. The settlement was to last until his bankruptcy or until he should suffer "something whereby the same would, by operation of law become payable to some other person". On such determination, the property was to be held on trust to pay the income to his wife. A judicial charge was created by a judgment made against him. Subsequently, the settlor was declared bankrupt. The wife was entitled to the income because, by the time he was bankrupt, his determinable interest had already ended. The judicial charge had operated as an involuntary alienation that ended the life interest.

Forfeiture

It is in the interests of the beneficiary with the determinable life interest (the principal beneficiary) to allege that forfeiture has taken place. On such an occurrence, his interest will not vest in the trustee in bankruptcy, but will instead be available for the beneficiaries under the discretionary trust.

The following offer illustrations as to the operation of forfeiture.

(a) In *Re Balfour's Settlement* (1938), the trustees had advanced money to a life tenant in breach of trust. The trustees asserted the right to retain future income to make good the breach of trust. The life tenant went bankrupt. It was held that the trustee in bankruptcy had no claim to the life interest as it had already determined.

(b) In *Re Gourins Will Trusts* (1943), the life tenant ceased to be entitled to receive the trust income because she lived in enemy territory during the Second World War. This amounted to a forfeiture. The discretionary trust came into operation, which entailed that the Custodian of Enemy Property could not claim her interest. Conversely, in *Re Hall* (1944), the Custodian was entitled. The trust expressly provided that forfeiture was only to operate if the beneficiary should "do or suffer any act" whereby the annuity should be payable elsewhere. As her failure to receive the annuity did not arise from her own act, but arose merely from the rules governing residents in enemy territory, there was no forfeiture.

(c) Under the Matrimonial Causes Act 1973, the High Court can make an order varying a protected life interest under a settlement. In *Re Richardson's Will Trusts* (1958), the court ordered that the beneficiary should charge his interest with an annual payment of £50 in favour of his ex-wife. It was held that this amounted to a forfeiture. By way of contrast, in *General Accident Fire and Life Assurance Corp Ltd v Inland Revenue Commission* (1963) an order of the court, diverting part of the income from a life tenant in favour of a former wife, did not amount to a forfeiture. As forfeiture is concerned with protecting a spendthrift life tenant against his creditors (and not against his former wife), the latter approach is thought to be preferable.

Discretionary trusts

Although in this context the purpose of discretionary trusts is to divert money after a determinable life interest has ended, discretionary trusts are widely employed elsewhere. They are important for exercising control over the young and improvident and to provide flexibility, say, when an employer seeks to provide benefits for employees.

The essence of a discretionary trust is that no single beneficiary has a right to any part of the income. The trustees have the discretion to distribute the trust fund as they think fit. Hence, and unless money has actually been paid to a beneficiary, there is no property that his creditors can claim: *Re Coleman* (1888).

9. RESULTING TRUSTS

These trusts are said to be "resulting" because, under such a trust, the beneficial interest in the property results back to the settlor or the settlor's estate. The resulting trust is a type of implied trust that arises by operation of law. Accordingly, it is not expressly created by a settlor. In *Re Vandervell's Trusts (No.2)* (1973), Megarry J. identified two types of resulting trust: the "automatic resulting trust" and the "presumed resulting trust". The latter is sometimes referred to as a "purchase money resulting trust".

Automatic resulting trust

This is a default mechanism that traditionally is viewed as having nothing to do with the intentions of the parties. Indeed, it can operate even where the transferor positively sought to dispose of his beneficial interest. Such a trust automatically arises in the following situations.

1. *Failure to declare a trust*. As in *Vandervell v Inland Revenue Commissioners* (1967), if the beneficial interest (there in an option to repurchase shares) is not dealt with then it will be held on resulting trust for the settlor. It would be rare for the court to conclude that the settlor had abandoned a beneficial interest and that it went to the Crown as a gift (*bona vacantia*).

2. *Incomplete disposal of the beneficial interest*. In *Re Cochrane* (1955), Harman J. described the resulting trust as, ". . .

the last resort to which the law has recourse when the drafts-
man has made a blunder or failed to dispose of that which he
has set out to dispose of.'' There, income paid to a wife under an
express trust had to be paid back to the husband's estate. A
resulting trust arose in favour of the estate because the express
trust had not completely dealt with the beneficial interest.

   3. Failure of an express trust.   Failure can occur for a
number of reasons. For example:

   (a) if the settlor has conveyed property on trust for A for life
       and made no other provision then on A's death the
       property would result back to the settlor or the settlor's
       estate;
   (b) if a settlor conveys property on trust for A for life and
       then to A's children absolutely, if A never has children
       the remainder will result back to the settlor;
   (c) where the trust turns out to be void because it is against
       public policy, advances an illegal purpose or offends the
       perpetuity rule;
   (d) in *Re Diplock* (1951), there was a gift of residue in a will
       "for purposes which the trustees consider to be charita-
       ble". This was not exclusively charitable and, therefore,
       was a private purpose trust that failed. The property
       resulted back to the settlor's estate and could be claimed
       by the grasping relatives.

   4. Surplus funds.   Complications can arise where an
express trust no longer continues (*e.g.* its purpose has been
achieved or it was established to benefit a non-charitable society
which has subsequently ceased to exist). If surplus money
remains, the central issue concerns what will happen to that
money. There are several alternative possibilities, one of which
is that the money might revert back to the settlor under the
auspices of a resulting trust. The outcome turns upon the
settlor's intentions as divined from the trust instrument and/or
surrounding circumstances:

   (a) in *Re Trusts of the Abbott Fund* (1900), money was collected
       for two deaf and dumb old ladies. This was not a
       charitable purpose and the women had no rights in the
       capital. Following their death, the surplus money was
       held on a resulting trust for those who donated the
       money.

(b) In *Re Andrews Trust* (1905), money was subscribed "for or towards" the education of the infant children of a deceased clergyman. On the completion of their education, the children were entitled to all the money in equal shares. A similar result was achieved in *Re Osoba* (1979) where a gift was made to the testator's widow "for her maintenance and for the training of my daughter up to university grade and for the maintenance of my aged mother". The mother predeceased the testator. The widow died and the daughter completed her education. It was held that the widow and the daughter took as joint tenants so that the daughter succeeded to the whole fund on the death of the widow. The references to education and maintenance were only explanations of the motive for the gift.

(c) In *Re Gillingham Bus Disaster Fund* (1958), a fund was set up following a disaster arising from a bus accident. The collection was for the injured survivors who were all naval cadets. The government declared that it would take over responsibility for the welfare of the cadets so that the purpose of the trust failed. It was held that the surplus money must result back to the subscribers. If the donors could not be found, the money was to be paid into court.

(d) In *Re Printers and Transferers Society* (1899), a society was founded to raise funds for industrial strikes and to provide benefits for strikers. The members of the society made weekly subscriptions to the fund. There was, however, no provision for what was to happen on the dissolution of the society. The court held there was a resulting trust for the existing members at the time of the dissolution. Similarly, in *Re Hobourne Aero Components Ltd's Air Raid Disaster Fund* (1946), the surplus funds were held on a resulting trust for anyone who had ever contributed according to his contribution, making allowance for any benefits received.

(e) In *Cunnack v Edwards* (1895), financial contributions to a society were viewed as an out-and-out transfer (*i.e.* a gift). On the dissolution of the society, there was no one to whom the surplus could go to by way of resulting trust. The surplus went to the Crown as *bona vacantia*.

(f) In *Re West Sussex Constabulary's Widows, Children and Benevolent Fund Trusts* (1971), money was received from donations, collecting boxes and proceeds from entertainment events. It was held that:

      (i) the money from identifiable donations should go back on a resulting trust;

     (ii) the money from collecting boxes was an outright gift and should go to the Crown as *bona vacantia*;

    (iii) the proceeds of the entertainment events should also go *bona vacantia*. Those who had purchased tickets had received what they had paid for and there was no question of them claiming the money back.

(g) In *Re Bucks Constabulary Widow's and Orphan's Fund Friendly Society* (1979), Walton J. held that voluntary subscriptions were an accretion to the funds of the society. They amounted to an outright gift. Hence, they should be distributed amongst those members who still belonged to the society at the date of dissolution. The modern tendency is to treat the rights of the members as being of a contractual nature without imposing a resulting trust: *Re Recher* (1972).

(h) In *Davis v Richards & Wallington Industries Ltd* (1991), however, this trend was not followed. While accepting that a resulting trust could be excluded expressly or by implication, Scott J. did not consider that a payment under a contract was in itself sufficient to exclude the operation of a resulting trust. There surplus funds derived from the employers' contributions to a pension fund were held on a resulting trust for the employer. As far as the employee's contributions were concerned, there was no resulting trust because it was impracticable to make the repayments. Those funds went to the Crown *bona vacantia*.

Presumed intention resulting trust

A presumed (or purchase money) resulting trust arises where property is purchased in the name of another or where there is a voluntary transfer or conveyance of property. Such a trust can arise in the following situations.

    1. *Purchase in the name of another*. The basic idea is that, if X buys property in the name of Y, a presumption arises that Y holds the property on resulting trust for X: *Dyer v Dyer* (1788). There will also be a resulting trust where two people together provide the purchase price, but the property is taken in the name of one of them only. For example, where the family home is conveyed only in the husband's name, but the wife had contributed to the purchase price. In such a case, he will hold the legal estate on trust for himself and his wife. In *Sekhon v Alissa* (1989), a mother and daughter purchased a house together, but title was transferred only in the daughter's name. The mother was entitled to a beneficial interest by reason of a resulting trust in proportion to the amount of her contribution.

The contribution must relate to the acquisition of the property. It may be *direct* as where one party pays either the deposit, conveyancing fees, stamp duty land tax, part of the balance of the purchase price or the mortgage instalments. It may be *indirect* as where one party pays other household expenses to enable the other to pay the mortgage instalments.

Not all types of contribution will, however, count. An interest will not be acquired merely by doing the housework and bringing up the children: *Burns v Burns* (1984). Similarly, carrying out improvements to the property will not suffice to trigger a resulting trust. A statutory exception to this rule operates as between spouses (but not cohabitants and same sex relationships). Under s.37 of the Matrimonial Proceedings and Property Act 1970, a substantial improvement made by a spouse can result in a share under an implied trust.

There must also be an intention on the part of the contributing party that he should have an interest in the property and, moreover, this must exist at the time of the purchase. This intention, however, need not be express and it can be inferred from conduct (even subsequent conduct): *Gissing v Gissing* (1971).

Under the Matrimonial Causes Act 1973, the courts have a wide discretion to redistribute property rights on divorce regardless of strict property principles. In other cases, the size and value of the shares must be ascertained. The beneficial interest under the resulting trust is proportionate to the contribution (*i.e.* you get back proportionally to what you put in). The exact valuation of the share will normally be calculated as at the date of the eventual sale.

2. *Voluntary transfer to another.* On the voluntary transfer of personalty there will be a resulting trust unless there is either an express intention to make a gift or the presumption of advancement applies. In *Re Vinogradoff* (1935), a grandmother made a lifetime transfer of £800 of War Loan shares to her young granddaughter. The transferor, however, continued to receive the dividends until her death. Subsequently, it was held that the granddaughter held the shares on resulting trust for the grandmother's estate. This case has been heavily criticised.

As regards transfers of land, s.60(3) of the Law of Property Act 1925 provides that,

> "In a voluntary conveyance a resulting trust for the grantor shall not be implied merely by reason that the property is not expressed to be conveyed for the use of benefit of the grantee."

Nevertheless, it is still possible to find a resulting trust where no gift was intended. In *Hodgson v Marks* (1971), Mrs Hodgson was persuaded to transfer her house to her lodger, Mr Evans, on the understanding that she would continue to be the beneficial owner. When he subsequently sold it to a purchaser, she was declared to have a beneficial interest under a resulting trust and, on the facts, this was binding on the purchaser.

The presumption of advancement

Sometimes the settlor will make it clear that he intends to make a gift of the property to the persons to whom it is conveyed. In relationships where the donor is under an obligation to provide for the donee, such an intention will be presumed. This is known as the rebuttable presumption of advancement. Much turns upon the exact nature of the relationship and the evidence placed before the court.

1. Wife. A husband who buys property and has it conveyed into the name of his wife, or who contributes to the mortgage payments in relation to property owned by her, is presumed to have intended a gift: *Silver v Silver* (1958). This presumption is, however, easily rebutted in modern times. It is also gender biased because if the wife contributes all the money and the property is conveyed into the name of the husband, there is no presumption of a gift. The husband will, in the absence of evidence to the contrary, be deemed to be holding on trust for her. This presumption applies also between fiance and fiancee: *Moate v Moate* (1948).

2. *Child.* If a father buys property and has it put into the name of his child then it is presumed he intended a gift: *Dyer v Dyer* (1788). The older cases indicate that there is no presumption of gift where a mother pays the purchase money and the property is in the name of the child: *Bennet v Bennet* (1879). This is because, in equity, there is no obligation on a mother to support her child.

3. Other relationships. The same presumption of advancement applies where someone has taken on the obligation of providing for a child, for example a stepson or a grandchild: *Re Paradise Motor Co Ltd* (1968). Although mothers are not caught by the previous head of advancement, it is thought that a widowed mother providing for her children would, at the least, fall within this category: *Re Grimes* (1937).

Rebutting the presumption

Both the presumption of a resulting trust and the presumption of advancement may be rebutted by evidence of a contrary intention. The court can take into account all the surrounding circumstances. For example, in the case of land an express declaration of trust will, in the absence of fraud, be conclusive. There will be no room for the presumption of either advancement or a resulting trust: *Goodman v Gallant* (1986).

(a) In *Warrent v Gurney* (1944), the presumption of advancement was rebutted in circumstances where a father bought a house which was conveyed into the name of his daughter. The father retained the deeds. On his death, the daughter claimed unsuccessfully to be the beneficial owner of the house. The retention of the deeds, coupled with other evidence at the time of the purchase, rebutted the intention to make a gift.

(b) Elderly parents might put their property into the names of their children for convenience where they do not want to be bothered with the legal formalities. In like vein, a father might not be able to obtain a mortgage in his own name and, therefore, may have to put the property in the name of a child. In these cases, the presumption of advancement would be rebutted: *Kyriakides v Pippas* (2004).

(c) Evidence of an illegal purpose cannot, however, be relied upon: *Tinsley v Milligan* (1993). The maxim "he who comes to equity must have clean hands" applies here. The House of Lords emphasised that a person cannot rely on his own fraud or illegality to rebut the presumption of advancement. It is necessary to show that the donor acted dishonestly: *Lavelle v Lavelle* (2004). In *Lowson v Coombs*

(1998), however, the artificiality of this rule was highlighted. There an illegal purpose existed, but as it was not necessary to rely on that evidence in order to succeed it was ignored. The illegality must, therefore, be invoked as evidence to justify the rebuttal of the presumption. For example, if a husband puts property into the name of a wife or a child in order to evade tax, he cannot then rely on this unlawful purpose in order to rebut the presumption of a gift: *Re Emery's Investment Trust* (1959). If the improper purpose is not carried into effect, however, the presumption of advancement may still be rebutted by showing the true reason for the transaction: *Tribe v Tribe* (1995). The area of illegality is under review and it is expected that Parliament will make it simply a matter for the discretion of the court whether or not to admit such evidence.

10. CONSTRUCTIVE TRUSTS

It is not possible to give an exhaustive definition of constructive trusts because they emerge in different forms with few common characteristics. Nevertheless, attempts are often made. For example, the definition approved by Edmund Davies L.J. in *Carl Zeiss Stiftung v Herbert Smith & Co (No.2)* (1967) is that,

> ". . . a constructive trust is a trust which is imposed by equity in order to satisfy the demands of justice and good conscience without reference to any express or presumed intention of the parties".

The traditional model

Where there is an existing fiduciary relationship, equity will, in some circumstances, impose a trust on persons who receive trust property. This is so even if they were not the trustees under the original trust. Similarly, a constructive trust may attach to additional property, for example, where existing trustees make a profit from the trust. The most important instances of this type of constructive trust are given below.

1. *Strangers to the trust.*

(a) Knowing receipt or dealing with trust property. A distinction must here be made between a liability *in rem* and personal liability.

   (i) Liability *in rem* means that a beneficiary has a proprietary remedy against a person who receives property in breach of trust. The beneficiary may recover the property from that person unless that person is a bona fide purchaser of a legal interest for value without notice of the breach of trust. Thus an innocent volunteer will be bound to restore any property (or its proceeds) that remain in his possession even though he had no knowledge of the breach of trust.

   (ii) Liability *in personam* allows a beneficiary to establish a personal liability, for example, where a stranger dealt with trust property, but never actually had it in his own hands. In such a case, the proprietary remedy would be of no assistance.

(b) It was once thought that a person would be liable as a constructive trustee only where, as Brightman J. put it in *Karak Rubber Co Ltd v Burden (No.2)* (1972):

   ". . . he has received trust property with *actual* or *constructive* notice that it is trust property transferred in breach of trust, or because (not being a bona fide purchaser for value without notice) he acquires notice subsequent to such receipt and then deals with the property in a manner inconsistent with the trust".

   In more recent cases, however, it has been said that liability should be based on "want of probity" (see *Re Montague's Settlement Trusts* (1987); *Eagle Trust plc v SBC Securities Ltd* (1991)).

(c) An agent will not be liable as a constructive trustee merely because he is in possession of property which he knows to be trust property: *Williams-Ashman v Price and Williams* (1942). He would of course be liable if he knew (or, possibly, ought to have known) that it was transferred to him in breach of trust.

(d) Where a solicitor incurs liability as a constructive trustee his partners will not be liable merely because money passes through the firm's client account: *Re Bell's Indenture* (1980). Any money, however, which remains in the account, can be recovered. A partner of the firm would be liable if he had notice of the breach of trust.

2. Accessory liability.   In this type of case, the property is not vested in the stranger. It is, therefore, incorrect to say that he is liable as a constructive trustee. Instead, he has a personal liability to account. In *Barnes v Addy* (1874), Lord Selbourne said that in order to be liable a stranger must have assisted "with knowledge in a dishonest and fraudulent design on the part of the trustees". This approach has, however, been rejected by the Privy Council in *Royal Brunei Airlines v Tan* (1995). There it was held that, where a third party dishonestly assisted a trustee to commit a breach of trust or procured him to do so, the third party would be liable irrespective of whether the trustee had been dishonest or fraudulent. Accessory liability is discussed further in Ch.18.

3. Profit from the trust.   A trustee must not profit from his trust. Any profit he does make will be held on a constructive trust for the beneficiaries. This is discussed in Ch.14 on trustees' duties.

4. Specifically enforceable contracts for sale.   Once a contract for the sale of land has been made, the beneficial ownership of the property passes to the purchaser and the vendor is deemed to hold the legal estate on a constructive trust for him. It is, however, a qualified trusteeship. This type of constructive trust is based upon the maxim "equity looks on that as done that ought to be done". The trustee is entitled to possession and to rents and profits until completion and is liable for expenses. Normally trustees are not entitled to profits but are entitled to reclaim expenses. Moreover, if the contract is never completed, it is as though the vendor never was a trustee so he cannot be made liable for breach of his trustee-type duties.

5. Mutual wills.   Mutual wills arise where two persons make an arrangement to make similar wills disposing of their property in a particular way. They must intend that the wills will be irrevocably binding on them. The mere fact that they leave similar wills is not enough. In *Re Oldham* (1925), a husband and wife left property to each other with the same provision should the other die first. There was no evidence that there was any arrangement or agreement that the wills should be irrevocable. After the husband died, the wife remarried and made another will. The second will was upheld.

An example of mutual wills is where under A's will property is left to B for life with remainder to C and under B's will property is left to A for life with remainder to C. On A's death, B is bound by the arrangement. Even if C dies before B, his estate will benefit because after the death of A the trust set up by B's will is irrevocable: *Re Haggar* (1930).

Either party can withdraw (subject to damages for breach of contract) from the mutual arrangement before the first death. Once the first person dies, however, the survivor holds the property on an implied or constructive trust for the beneficiaries named in the will. If the survivor makes a second will, his personal representatives (under the new version) will hold the property on the trusts of the first will. It is not necessary that the second testator to die should have obtained a personal financial benefit under the will of the first testator to die: *Re Dale's Estate* (1993). The normal rule that marriage revokes a will does not affect the trust: *Re Goodchild* (1996). Where there are mutual wills, therefore, a floating trust is created which will not be overturned by the second testator's remarriage: *Goodman v Goodman* (1996).

There may be difficulties in establishing what property is bound by the trust. The wills themselves may make the position clear. If not, it may be that the trust covers only the property that the survivor receives from the estate of the first to die. Alternatively, it may include that property as well as the property that the survivor owned at that time or, indeed, even the property that the survivor owned when he died. In *Re Cleaver* (1981), it was held that a survivor could in his lifetime enjoy the property as an absolute owner "subject to a fiduciary duty which, so to speak, crystallised on his death and disabled him only from voluntary dispositions *inter vivos*".

6. Secret trusts. As discussed in Ch.6, some writers treat secret trusts as constructive trusts.

7. Conveyance by fraud. Where there is a lifetime conveyance that is induced by fraud, the transferee may be held to hold the property as a constructive trustee for the transferor or some third party: *Rochefoucauld v Boustead* (1897).

Constructive trusts and the family home

Many of the cases in which a constructive trust is invoked focus upon informal family arrangements that go awry. There are two key House of Lords decisions concerning what is known as the "common intention constructive trust" in this context:

1. In *Gissing v Gissing* (1970), the House of Lords considered the essentials for establishing a constructive trust as being:

(a) that at the time the property is acquired the parties must have intended that the non-legal owner should have a beneficial interest; and

(b) that the non-legal owner should have made a contribution to the property or acted in some way to his detriment in the belief that he had such an interest.

2. This approach was amplified in *Lloyds Bank v Rosett* (1990), where Lord Bridge restated the law and identified two rules under which a non-legal owner of land can acquire an equitable interest in the family home.

(a) **Rule 1** of *Rosett* relates to express bargains and applies where there has been a discussion about property rights between the parties, and consequently some arrangement, agreement or understanding has been reached. Where there is some express agreement, there is no scope for a resulting trust (see Ch.9). Some further points need to be noted:

   (i) the claimant must have acted to his detriment (or significantly altered his position) in reliance upon that arrangement and if so either a constructive trust or a proprietary estoppel will be invoked;

   (ii) detriment is not limited merely to financial contributions to the purchase of the property and can encompass moving house, giving up work, housekeeping and looking after children, for example;

   (iii) the trust or estoppel will be employed to give effect to the express and shared intention. This intention needs to be express and communicated: *Springette v Defoe* (1992). As Steyn L.J. admitted, "our trust law does not allow property rights to be affected by telepathy". Following *Hammond v Mitchell* (1991), it is necessary that the express discussions alleged should be pleaded in detail;

   (iv) the rule is, however, arbitrary as it depends solely upon whether there was a discussion or not. If no discussion has taken place, the rule simply does not apply: *Burns v Burns* (1984). In *Eves v Eves* (1975), where a cohabiting couple bought a house that was conveyed into the sole name of the male partner. His reason for this was that the woman, with whom he lived, was under 21 years of age. They had two children together and she undertook much work in the house and garden before he left her. The Court of Appeal held she was entitled to a quarter share. Similarly, in *Grant v Edwards* (1985), the Court of Appeal found for the woman where a false reason was given for the house not being put in joint names. In the expectation of acquiring a beneficial interest, the woman had made substantial contributions to the family expenses. She acquired a half share of the family home. More recently, in *Drake v Whipp* (1996) Mr Whipp had promised Mrs Drake that her name would eventually be put on the legal title to the barn conversion, but he repeatedly claimed to be too busy to attend to the matter. As she had clearly acted to her detriment in reliance on the agreement, a constructive trust arose.

(v) In *Clough v Killey* (1996), Peter Gibson L.J. admitted that, where there is an express understanding and shares are agreed (*e.g.* that the property will be divided 50/50), ". . .it is only common sense that . . . those shares *prima facie* are the shares to which the court will give effect". The court could depart from this rule only when there was good cause to do so. In *Drake v Whipp* (1996), however, the shares were left unspecified. The court felt it necessary to look at all the circumstances, including contributions to the running of the home and family, to determine what constituted a fair share. In *Grant v Edwards* (1986), this involved taking into account indirect assistance such as the payment of household expenses, contributions by way of labour and other actions of the claimant.

(b) **Rule 2** of *Rosett* covers implied bargains and applies where there has been no express discussion between the parties. In this situation, the court looks in detail at their conduct with the prospect of presuming a common intention to share beneficial ownership. If the intention to share is inferred, a constructive trust will arise. The beneficiary's share under this trust will be calculated in the light of all the circumstances.

For the trust to arise, however, the claimant must have made some *direct* financial contribution either to the (initial or on-going) purchase of the property. If only *indirect* contributions are present (*e.g.* looking after children, paying household expenses, financing improvements, decorating, and labour), there will be no ground to justify the inference of a common intention to acquire a beneficial share: *Burns v Burns* (1984).

Once the constructive trust is invoked, however, the court can look beyond the direct contributions that underpin its existence and calculate a share that, on the facts of each case, reflects the overall contribution made. On occasion, as in *Midland Bank v Cooke* (1995), the court may adopt a broader test of what is fair and just.

Distinguishing from a resulting trust

1. In *McKenzie v McKenzie* (2003), the High Court attempted to distinguish between constructive and resulting trusts. The court concluded that a constructive trust arises out of, and is equity's way of giving effect to, the common intentions of the parties. It is equity's method of enforcing conscience. In contrast, a resulting trust is equity's response to the failure of a gift or proof of lack of common intention to make one. As regards a resulting trust, the basis for equity's intervention is not proof of a common intention, but a presumption that a person is unlikely to have paid for property altruistically without some expectation of return (see Ch.9).

2. As regards a resulting trust, the existence of the trust is established once and for all at the date on which the property is acquired. The shares crystallise at that point and subsequent contributions traditionally do not count.

3. As to the quantification of the beneficial interest, different rules apply according to whether the implied trust is resulting or constructive. In relation to the former, the claimant should obtain a share commensurate with the value of the contribution. It is a mathematically driven approach. In the case of a constructive trust, quantification should, when possible, be according to what the parties intended.

11. NON-CHARITABLE PURPOSE TRUSTS

1. *The beneficiary principle*. For a trust to be valid it must have a human beneficiary by whom the trust can be enforced: *Morice v Bishop of Durham* (1804). Private purpose trusts are sometimes called trusts of imperfect obligation because the trustees are not strictly obliged to carry out the trust in the absence of an enforcer.

The general rule is that private purpose trusts are void: *Re Astor* (1952). This has become known as "the beneficiary principle". In that case a trust for "the maintenance of good understanding between nations and the preservation and integrity of newspapers" was held invalid. There was no human beneficiary who could police the trust. It was too abstract and too impersonal. In *Re Shaw* (1957), a trust to promote a new 40-letter alphabet was void. The trust was not charitable and it had no beneficiary to enforce it.

2. *Charitable trusts*. As the rule is limited to private trusts, where the purpose of the trust is charitable the absence of a human beneficiary is not fatal. A charitable trust can, where necessary, be enforced by the Attorney General (see Ch.12).

3. *Perpetuity*. The operation of the rule against perpetuities has relevance in relation to pure purpose trusts and gifts for unincorporated associations. The perpetuity rule is concerned with the duration for which a settlor can tie up property. The rule is that any future interest in the property must vest within 21 years of the death of some named person (or persons) alive the date of the disposition. If a period is not specified, the court will usually confine the duration of the gift to 21 years. An alternative is offered by the Perpetuities and Accumulations Act 1964 that allows the settlor to choose a fixed period not exceeding 80 years. As regards unincorporated associations, care as to be taken if the funds are to benefit future (as well as present) members. In such an instance, the gift must be structured so as to end within the perpetuity period.

As regards a true purpose trust (*e.g.* to maintain a tomb or animals), the 80-year rule is thought not to apply: s.15(4). The perpetuity period will be either 21 years or geared to a life (or lives) in being.

Purpose trusts: anomalous exceptions

There are some odd cases where a trust has been upheld even though it clearly advances a private purpose. If a pure purpose trust is upheld, it is essential that the trustee must give an undertaking to perform the trust. If the funds are misapplied by the trustee, those entitled to the residuary estate can complain to the court. These exceptional cases were decided before *Re Astor* (1952) and, based upon a dubious foundation, are unlikely to be followed in modern times. Indeed, in *Re Endacott* (1960), these exceptions were described as ". . . troublesome, anomalous and aberrant." There the Court of Appeal held as void a gift of £20,000 for the provision of a "useful monument to myself".

1. *Maintenance of specific animals.* In *Pettingall v Pettingall* (1842), a trust of £50 to look after the testator's favourite mare for 50 years was upheld. In *Re Dean* (1889), a gift of £750 per annum to maintain the testator's horses, ponies and hounds "if they should so long live" was held to be valid.

2. *Trusts for erection and maintenance of monuments.* In *Pirbright v Salwey* (1896), £800 was given to the rector of the parish to use the income for the upkeep of a grave. This case was followed in *Re Hooper* (1932) which concerned the upkeep of family tombs and monuments. Similarly, in *Mussett v Bingle* (1876), £300 was left to erect a monument to the first husband of the testator's wife was valid. Maintenance of private graves is now possible for 99 years under s.1 of the Parish Council and Burial Authorities (Miscellaneous Provisions) Act 1970.

3. *Trusts for masses.* In *Bourne v Keane* (1919), a trust for the saying of private masses for an individual was held valid by the House of Lords. Note that masses open to the public are categorised as charitable: *Re Hetherington* (1989).

4. *Promotion and furtherance of foxhunting.* In *Re Thompson* (1934), a trust to promote these purposes was upheld on the facts. Not surprisingly, the decision has never been followed.

Purpose trusts and the *Denley* principle

In *Re Denley's Trust Deed* (1969), a trust to provide a recreation ground for the benefit of employees of a company was viewed as a valid trust because the employees were a class of beneficiaries with sufficient standing to enforce the trust. It was not a pure purpose trust. Goff J. explained,

> ". . . when, then, the trust though expressed as a purpose, is directly or indirectly for the benefit of an individual or individuals, it seems to me that it is in general outside the mischief of the beneficiary principle."

In *R. v District Auditor, Ex p. West Yorkshire Metropolitan County Council* (1986), it was held that, if the class of potential beneficiaries is too large, there are no ascertainable beneficiaries to fall within the *Denley* principle.

Unincorporated associations

In *Conservative and Unionist Central Office v Burrell* (1982) an unincorporated association was said to exist where:

(i) two or more persons are bound together;
(ii) for one (or more) common purpose(s);
(iii) by mutual undertakings, each having mutual duties and obligations;
(iv) in an organisation which has rules identifying in whom control of the organisation and its funds is vested; and
(v) which can be joined or left at will.

The main problem about gifts to an unincorporated association is that it does not have a distinct legal entity (as an individual or a company does) which can hold the property. Hence, a gift to an unincorporated association can be construed in several ways.

Neville v Madden

1. As a gift to present members of the association at the date of the gift as joint tenants or tenants in common. The members could if they wanted divide the property between themselves, each taking a share. This was the construction put upon a gift in *Cocks v Manners* (1871) where a testator left a share of his residue to the Dominican Convent at Carisbrooke "payable to the superior for the time being".

2. As a gift to trustees (or other proper officers of the committee) for the purposes of the association. On this construction the gift would fail for lack of a human beneficiary. In *Leahy v Att-Gen (New South Wales)* (1959), a gift of a sheep station for "such order of nuns of the Catholic Church or the Christian brothers as my trustees shall select" was held not to be a gift for individual members of the order.

3. As a gift to the members, not as joint tenants, but subject to their respective contractual rights and liabilities towards one another as members of the association. In such a case, a member cannot sever his share. It will accrue to the others on his death or resignation, even though such members include persons who became members after the gift took effect: *Neville Estates v Madden* (1962).

(a) In *Re Rechers Will Trusts* (1972), Brightman L.J. favoured a contractual approach:

> ". . . in the absence of words which purport to impose a trust, the legacy is a gift to the members beneficially, not as joint tenants or as tenants in common so as to entitle each member to an immediate beneficial share, but as an accretion to the funds which are the subject matter of the contract which the members have made *inter se*."

(b) In *Re Lipinski's Will Trust* (1976), The testator left part of his residuary estate to the Hull Judeans (Maccabi) Association "to be used solely in the work of constructing the new buildings for the association and for improvements to the said building". It was held that the gift was not a pure purpose trust and was, instead, for the benefit of ascertainable beneficiaries. The trust was valid because the members of the association had the power to alter the purpose for which the money could be used and could divide the money between themselves.

(c) If, however, the members of the association have no control over the funds the trust will fail. In *Re Grants Will Trusts* (1980), there was a trust for the purposes of the Chertsey Labour Party Headquarters. There the members did not control the property nor could they change their constitution to enable them to do so.

(d) On the dissolution of an unincorporated association, the funds are distributed to reflect how the members held the property in the first place: *Re Bucks Constabulary Fund (No.2)* (1979). There was in that case an equal distribution of the funds between the surviving members (to the exclusion of former members) in line with the contract holding theory.

4. As a gift to members of the association imposing on them a mandate to apply the property for the purposes of the association. This is possible for a gift *inter vivos,* but not a testamentary disposition (there can be no agency between the deceased and the association). This possibility was suggested by Brightman L.J. in *Conservative and Unionist Central Office v Burrell (Inspector of Taxes)* (1982).

Powers for purposes

If the gift is drafted as a power rather than a trust, it will remain valid even if there is no human beneficiary. The beneficiary principle does not apply to powers because the donee of a power cannot be compelled to exercise it. In *Re Shaw* (1957), a trust to promote the advantages of a new alphabet failed as a trust, but Harman J. indicated that, if had been drafted as a power, it might have succeeded. A valid power will not, however, be spelled out of an invalid trust: *Inland Revenue Commissioners v Broadway Cottages* (1955).

12. CHARITABLE TRUSTS

Charitable trusts are public trusts. They are usually designed to promote a purpose that is beneficial to society. A charitable trust may also be framed so as to benefit a particular charitable organisation (which can be a company or an unincorporated association). As will be shown, the attraction of achieving charitable status is that it brings with it a variety of fiscal and legal privileges.

It is, therefore, surprising then that there is no statutory definition of charity and its meaning has to be derived from case law and decisions of Charity Commissioners. This is because, as the House of Lords admitted in *Inland Revenue Commissioners v Baddeley* (1955), ". . . there is no limit to the number and diversity of ways in which man will seek to benefit his fellow men''. The Nathan Committee Report (1952) concluded that a strict definition was neither possible nor desirable. In 2003, the government accepted that the current understanding of what amounts to charity is deficient and proposed that new charities legislation be enacted. This would contain a number of specific purposes that would be charitable and these are listed at the end of this chapter. There will, however, be no exhaustive, all embracing definition.

Advantages of charitable status

1. *Enforceability.* Charitable trusts do not require ascertainable beneficiaries to enforce them. They are enforceable by the Attorney-General. The Charity Commissioners have administrative responsibilities and can exercise powers of enforcement with the consent of the Attorney General: s.32 Charities Act 1993.

2. *Certainty.* Provided that the donor has shown a clear intention that the property be applied for charitable purposes, it does not matter that he fails to choose a specific named charity. The court will draw up a scheme for division of the property to charities. In *Moggridge v Thackwell* (1803), the testatrix left her residuary property to a trustee to dispose of to charities as he thought fit. She recommended clergymen with large families and good character. The trustee predeceased the testatrix and the next-of-kin claimed the property. The court held that the property be applied exclusively to charity, even though the testatrix had not specified particular charitable objects. Provided that the objects are wholly and exclusively charitable, the courts or the Charity Commissioners can remedy any vagueness by preparing a scheme for the application of funds.

3. *Perpetuity.* A gift must vest in a charity within the perpetuity period. Once so vested, however, a gift over to another charity can occur outside the perpetuity period; the vesting being for charitable purposes it does not matter that the actual charity is changed subsequently, *Christ's Hospital v Grainger* (1849). As a charity is not subject to the rule against inalienability, capital may be tied up indefinitely.

4. *Tax advantages.* The main advantage of charitable status is the privileged tax position that it attracts. For example:

(i) a charity does not pay tax on income that is applied solely for charitable purposes. Profits from a trade carried on by a charity, however, are non-taxable only if the trade is exercised in the course of the carrying out of a primary purpose of the charity or the work is mainly carried out by the beneficiaries of the charity;

(ii) gifts made to charities are exempt from Inheritance Tax and there is no Capital Gains Tax on a gain made by a charity that is applied solely for charitable purposes;

(iii) all charities are entitled to 80 per cent council tax relief where land is occupied by or used by a charity and wholly or mainly used for charitable purposes. Further relief is at the discretion of the local authority.

The legal understanding of charity

Some guidance as to what amounts to charity can be derived from the Preamble to the Statute of Charitable Uses 1601. This does not provide an exhaustive list, but represents a general catalogue of purposes regarded as charitable at that time. Although repealed by the Charities Act 1960, this list is still thought to exert some influence when the court or the commissioners are faced with new types of potentially charitable activity.

The Preamble read as follows:

> "The relief of aged, impotent and poor people, the maintenance of sick and maimed soldiers and mariners, schools of learning, free schools and scholars in universities; the repair of bridges, ports, havens, causeways, churches, sea banks and highways; the education and preferment of orphans; the relief, stock or maintenance for houses of correction; the marriage of poor maids, the supportation aid and help of young tradesmen, handicraftsmen and persons decayed; the relief or redemption of prisoners or captives; the aid or ease of any poor inhabitants concerning payment of fifteens, setting out of soldiers and other taxes."

1. *The four heads of charity.* The major case is *Commissioners for Special Purposes of Income Tax v Pemsel* (1891) where Lord McNaughten established the four heads of charity: the relief of poverty; the advancement of education; the advancement of religion; and other purposes beneficial to the community. It is, however, possible for a purpose to fall within more than one of the headings. If a purpose falls under one of the four heads of charity it is said to be "inherently charitable" or of "inherent benefit".

2. *Public benefit.* In order to be charitable, the purpose must also benefit of the public or a sufficient section of the public. A "public benefit test" is applied, but the nature of the test varies according to which head of charity is being considered.

3. *Exclusively charitable.* The final requirement is that the purpose must be "exclusively charitable". Accordingly, where a gift is given for a number of specific purposes it will not be a valid charitable trust unless all the purposes are charitable. For example, in *Re Ward* (1941), a gift for educational, or charitable or religious purposes was held to be valid because each of the heads was exclusively charitable. In *Morice v Bishop of Durham* (1805), a gift for benevolent purposes was held not to be exclusively charitable. Phrases such as "charitable *or* benevolent", "charitable *or* deserving" and so on have been held to lack the necessary exclusivity. The word "or" imports an alternative and is said to be disjunctive. Indeed, the outcome may often turn upon the presence or absence of punctuation. For example, in *Re Eades* (1920), references were made to "religious, charitable and philanthropic" purposes. The use of comma after religious indicated that each class was separate and disjunctive and, therefore, it was not exclusively charitable.

Conversely, in *Re Sutton* (1885), a gift for "charitable *and* deserving" purposes was held to be valid. In *Re Best* (1904), "charitable *and* benevolent" was held to be exclusively charitable. Although both "deserving" and "benevolent" are open to a non-charitable meaning, in both cases the words were linked to an overt charitable purpose by use of the word "and".

There are some situations where the rule that the gift must be exclusively charitable will not apply.

(a) If an executor or trustee is directed to divide property between charitable and non-charitable objects the trust will not wholly fail. In default of apportionment, the court will divide the fund equally and the trust will be valid as to the charitable half: *Salusbury v Denton* (1857).

(b) It does not matter if a trust for charitable purposes incidentally benefits objects that are not charitable. In *Re Coxen* (1948), the fact that a testator directed that £100 of a charitable fund of £200,000 could be used for a dinner for the trustees did not stop the trust from being exclusively charitable.

(c) Trusts to benefit a country or a particular locality may be interpreted by the courts as being limited exclusively to charitable purposes. This cannot occur, however, if the donor has spelt out the purposes, some of which are non-charitable: *Houston v Burns* (1918).

Relief of poverty

1. Inherent benefit?

(a) Poverty is not limited to destitution and, in *Re Coulthurst* (1951), was equated with persons who have to "go short". A gift to be applied for widows and orphaned children of deceased officers of Coutts & Company's Bank was upheld as being charitable. In *Garfield Poverty Trust* (1995), it was held that those who could not afford to take on a mortgage could be classified as being "poor" and, hence, the provision of interest free loans to buy houses was charitable.

(b) Gifts have been upheld even when the poorest have been excluded. In *Re De Carteret* (1933), an annuity of £40 to widows and spinsters, whose annual income would otherwise be not less than £8 or no more than £120, was upheld.

(c) It is not necessary that the words "poverty" or "poor" be employed. For example, in *Re Scarisbrick* (1951) the expression "in needy circumstances" indicated poverty. Similarly, in *Re Gardom* (1914) the expression "of limited means" was sufficient. In R*e Cohen* (1919), however, the term "deserving" did not connote a sufficient need and was outside the first head of charity.

(d) Poverty may also be inferred from the nature of the gift. In *Biscoe v Jackson* (1887) the provision of a soup kitchen qualified under the head of poverty. In *Re Gosling* (1900), the provision of a superannuation fund for "pensioning off old worn out clerks" was viewed as being implicitly for the relief of poverty. A borderline example is *Re Niyazi* (1978) where the construction of a working men's hostel in Cyprus was held to be charitable.

2. *Public benefit?* It is arguable that there is no public benefit test whatsoever that applies to poverty. If such a test exists, however, it is hardly demanding. This leniency is explained on basis that the relief of poverty is so altruistic that a public benefit element can be necessarily inferred. Accordingly, a trust for a testator's poor relations is charitable: *Isaac v Defriez* (1754). Similarly, in *Re Gosling* (1900) poor employees were permitted to benefit.

It still remains necessary to distinguish between a private trust and a public (*i.e.* charitable) trust. In *Re Scarisbrick* (1951), the distinction was drawn between a trust to benefit named poor relations (a private trust) and a trust to benefit unnamed poor relations (a public trust). In *Re Segelman* (1996), however, a gift to poor and needy members of a class of six named relatives and their descendants (who totalled 26 persons on the testator's death) was upheld. Presumably, this was saved because the majority of potential beneficiaries were unnamed.

3. *Exclusively charitable?* It is also necessary that a trust to relieve poverty is exclusively charitable. A trust will not be for the relief of poverty if it can benefit the rich as well as the poor. In *Re Gwyon* (1930), a trust to establish a clothing foundation to provide clothing to boys in Farnham floundered because it failed to exclude more affluent children. The case demonstrates that benefits must be restricted to the poor.

Advancement of education

1. *Inherent benefit?* Education is not restricted to formal education in educational institutions such as schools and universities. It is, however, necessary that there is some element of instruction or improvement. In addition, there must be more than simply an accumulation of knowledge. In *Re Shaw* (1957), the settlor directed his trustees to use his residuary estate for a number of specified purposes. These included the devising of a new 40-letter alphabet and the translation of some of plays into that new alphabet. It was held not to be charitable because there was ". . . no element of teaching or education".

In *Re Hopkin's Will Trust* (1965) the testatrix bequeathed some of her residuary estate to the Francis Bacon Society. This was to be applied towards discovering evidence of Bacon's authorship of plays usually accredited to Shakespeare. Upholding the charitable nature of this trust, Wilberforce J. held that research can be regarded as charitable when it is worthwhile (unlike in *Re Shaw*) and will lead to something which will pass into the store of educational material.

The concept of education clearly includes formal teaching, including the study or promotion of individual subjects. For example, the study of Egyptology (*Re British School of Egyptian Archaeology* (1954)); the general advancement of mechanical science (*Institute of Civil Engineers v Inland Revenue Commissioners* (1932)); and typing and bookkeeping (*Re Koettgen's Will Trust* (1954)).

Education extends to the provision of educational public services and is wide enough to include forms of worthwhile instruction and cultural advancement. For example, the provision of botanical gardens, museums, libraries and choirs. Indeed, in *Incorporated Council of Law Reporting v Att-Gen* (1972) the preparation of law reports was held to be charitable.

In *Re Delius* (1957), the wife of the composer Delius gave her residuary estate for the advancement of her late husband's work. This was held to be charitable because the trust was to spread knowledge and appreciation of Delius' work throughout the world. In *Re Pinion* (1965), however, an artist left his studio and its contents to trustees to enable it to be used as a museum to display his collection of works. Harman L.J. admitted,

> "I can see of no useful object to be served in foisting upon the public this mass of junk. It has neither public utility nor educational value".

It was held not to be charitable. A similar stance was adopted in *Re Hummeltenberg* (1923) where a college for the training of spiritualist mediums not charitable.

Trusts to advance sports as such are not charitable. In *Re Nottage* (1895), a trust to provide a cup for yachting was not charitable. If, however, the sports are at a school then it will be charitable. In *Re Mariette* (1915), there was a valid charitable trust to provide squash courts at Aldenham School and a prize for athletics. The sporting facilities do not necessarily have to be at a particular school. In *Inland Revenue Commissioner v McMullen* (1981), a trust to provide facilities for soccer at schools and universities in the UK was held to assist the physical education and development of the young.

2. Public benefit? There must be a genuine public benefit in educational trusts. The law is anxious that educational trusts should not be used as a tax avoidance measure to provide education for the wealthy at the expense of the taxpayer. Similarly, the law will not allow employers to gain commercial advantage by setting up educational trusts for the children of their employees. Hence, in *Re Compton* (1945) a trust providing for the education of the descendants of three named persons was not a valid charitable trust. As the beneficiaries were defined by reference to a personal relationship, the trust lacked any public element.

In *Oppenheim v Tobacco Securities Trust Co Ltd* (1951), the House of Lords approved a test that has become known as "the blood and contract rule" or "personal nexus test". There, money was given to provide education for the children of employees of the British American Tobacco Corporation and its subsidiaries. The number of employees exceeded 110,000. It was held that, even with these large numbers, the personal nexus between the employers and employees meant that there was not a sufficient public benefit. Lord MacDermott, however, dissented. He considered that the public benefit question should be one of degree depending on the facts of the particular case.

Attempts are sometimes made to side-step the blood and contract rule. In *Re Koettgen's Will Trust* (1954), a trust was established to further the education of British born persons, with a direction that preference be given to employees of a particular company in respect of 75 per cent of fund. The trust was held to be primarily for the public, a mere preference being given to employee's families. This decision is open to question and appears to undermine the policy underlying the blood and contract rule. In *Inland Revenue Commissioners v Educational Grants Association Ltd* (1967), however, a trust to advance education was set up by the Metal Box Company. The evidence showed that over 75 per cent of the payments made went towards the education of children connected to the company. The trust was held not to be charitable.

In *Southwood v Att-Gen* (2000), a project on demilitarisation based at Bradford University failed. Although the objective of peace was uncontroversial, the objective of this trust was to be achieved by challenging the policies of western governments. It was merely political propaganda and, therefore, not in the public benefit. As will be shown, political trusts are never charitable.

3. Exclusively charitable? A further difficulty with *Southwood v Att-Gen* (2000) was that the political dimension of the trust prevented it being exclusively educational in nature. Similarly, in *Re Hopkinson* (1949) a trust to educate the public in the aims of a political party (Labour) could not be charitable because it amounted to political propaganda and was not exclusively educational. However, in, *Att-Gen v Ross* (1986), a gift to London Polytechnic Students Union was charitable even though it had ancillary non-charitable purposes (*e.g.* providing shops and a bar).

Advancement of religion

1. *Inherent benefit?* The law draws no distinction between one religion and another and adopts the view that any religion is better than none: *Neville Estates v Madden* (1962). The courts feel ill equipped to make value judgments on the inherent benefit of particular religious beliefs: *Holmes v AG* (1981) which concerned the Sun Myung Moon Foundation (the "Moonies"). For example, in *Thornton v Howe* (1862) a trust for the publication of the works of Joanna Southcote was held to be charitable. She claimed that she had been impregnated by the Holy Ghost and would give birth to the second Messiah. Charitable status will be refused to any religion that is deemed to be subversive of morality, contrary to the public interest or adverse to the very foundations of all religion. The worship of Satan or the promotion of black magic cannot be charitable. Paganism and trusts for the promotion of paganism have also not been viewed with favour.

For a religion to exist there has to be some belief in the existence of some Supreme Being and the worship of that being. In *Re South Place Ethical Society* (1980), the society existed to cultivate "rational religious sentiment". It was, however, an agnostic society interested in ethical and rational principles charitable status was denied. Dillon J. explained, "Religion is concerned with man's relations with God and ethics are concerned with man's relations with man."

The general tendency is, therefore, to give a broad interpretation of what can constitute religion for charitable purposes. In *Re le Cren Clarke* (1996), promotion of faith healing amongst a religious group was upheld. In *Power, Praise and Healing Mission* (1976), a trust for the advancement of religion by means including exorcism was granted charitable status.

Gifts to repair a church, to provide a stained glass window, to finance the purchase of an organ and to train clergy, for example, will fall within this head of charity.

2. *Public benefit?* The religion must benefit a sufficient section of the community. This rule is illustrated by *Gilmour v*

Coates (1949) where property was left on trust for a Carmelite convent. The Carmelites are a contemplative order who do not venture outside the convent walls. It was concluded that prayer and spiritual belief alone were of no tangible benefit to the public. In contrast, *The Society of the Precious Blood* (1995) concerned Anglican nuns and this was held to be charitable. These nuns were not cut off from the outside world. They worked in the community as well as providing classes and talks. Unlike *Gilmour*, this obviously had a public benefit.

The provision of a retreat house may be charitable if it is open to the public: *Neville Estates v Madden* (1962). A gift for private masses is not charitable. A gift for masses for the dead has, however, been held to have sufficient public benefit when the mass is part of a public ritual: *Re Hetherington* (1990). Similarly, a gift to maintain an individual tomb lacks public benefit, but the maintenance of all the tombs in a churchyard is charitable: *Doe d Thompson v Pritcher* (1815).

3. *Exclusively charitable?* As shown, a charitable purpose might be linked with another purpose and it is then necessary to look at wording used. If the gift is limited to, for example, the office of a priest or vicar, it will be deemed to be exclusively charitable: *Re Rumball* (1956) (a bishop). In *Farley v Westminster Bank* (1939), however, a gift to a vicar "for parish work" was not viewed as being a gift for his work as a vicar in the parish. As it was not directly linked to his office as vicar, it embraced non-charitable purposes.

Other purposes beneficial to the community

1. *Inherent benefit?* This fourth head of charity represents a ragbag of worthy causes that have been recognised as being charitable. It is not as straightforward as the other heads of charity because not all purposes beneficial to the community will be classified as being charitable. The orthodox view is that the purposes must be specified in (or, at least, analogous to those purposes) the 1601 Preamble. It is sometimes said that the purpose must fall within the spirit and intendment of the Preamble. For example, in *Re Strakosch* (1949) a trust to promote unity between the UK and South Africa was denied charitable status. While it could be said to benefit the community, it did not match any of the purposes as set out in the Preamble.

Although our understanding of what benefits the public has changed dramatically since 1601, judges appear ready to discover an example from which to draw an analogy. For example, in *Vancouver Regional Freenet Association v Minister of National Revenue* (1996) charitable status was given to a society whose object was the provision of free public access to the Internet. The court drew an analogy between the information highway and the repair of highways highlighted in the Preamble. Both intended to improve communications.

In *Council of Law Reporting for England and Wales v Att-Gen* (1972), Russell L.J. offered an alternative approach. He said that if the purpose cannot be viewed as anything other than being beneficial to the community, it should be charitable unless there is any reason for holding it not to be so.

Examples of charitable purposes under the fourth head include:

(i) a gift for a Fire Brigade (*Re Wokingham Fire Brigade Trusts* (1951));

(ii) gifts for the increased efficiency or morale of the army (*Re Good* (1905));

(iii) gifts for the promotion of industry, commerce and art (*Crystal Palace Trustees v Minister of Town & Country Planning* (1950));

(iv) trusts for the promotion of sport in the army: *Re Gray* (1925);

(iv) trusts to promote physical wellbeing: *e.g.* to provide guide dogs, to build hospitals, to protect vulnerable children, to prevent alcoholism and drug abuse and to offer family planning advice;

(vi) trusts for the protection of animals generally will be upheld if they promote and encourage human kindness: *Re Wedgewood* (1915). In *Re Grove-Grady* (1929), however, a sanctuary for animals or birds to keep them safe from molestation by man was not a charitable purpose. The court could discern no benefit in stopping people becoming involved with animals;

(vii) Social and recreational purposes have caused difficulties. In *Inland Revenue Commissioners v Baddeley* (1955), a controversy arose over a trust for the promotion of the religious, social and physical well being of the Methodists of West Ham and Leyton. It failed, in part, because social purposes were not charitable. This decision led to the passing of the Recreational Charities Act 1958 which provides that it is charitable to provide, or assist in the provision of facilities for recreation or other leisure-time occupation, if the facilities are provided in the interests of social welfare. This requires that the facilities be provided with the object of improving the conditions of life for the persons for whom the facilities are primarily intended. In addition, either the persons have need of these facilities by reason of youth, age, infirmity or disablement, poverty or social and economic circumstances; or the facilities are to be available to the members of the public at large. The Act specifically covers:

> "facilities at village halls, community centres and women's institutes, and to the provision and maintenance of grounds and buildings to be used for purposes of recreation and leisure-time occupation."

2. Public benefit? In many of the examples of gifts considered to fall under this fourth head of charity, the gift is for the potential benefit of the whole public. It does not matter that only a limited number of people will actually take advantage of it. For example, the provision of a bridge is a charitable purpose provided that it is available for everyone to use. It does not lose charitable status simply because only a few people decide to use it. It will not be charitable, however, if the use of the bridge is confined to a selected number of persons, no matter how large that number is. This is called "the class within a class rule."

In *Inland Revenue Commissioners v Badderley* (1955), a trust was established to promote the moral, social and physical wellbeing of persons resident in West Ham who were members of the Methodist Church. The House of Lords held that this was not charitable under the fourth head. The distinction was drawn between a benefit that is extended to the whole community (even though advantageous only to a few) and relief accorded to a selected few out of a larger number. Viscount Simmonds explained,

> "... the beneficiaries are a class within a class; they are those of the inhabitants of a particular area who are members of a particular church ... a trust cannot qualify as a charity within the fourth class ... if the beneficiaries are a class of persons not only confined to a particular area but selected from within it by reference to a particular creed."

Political trusts are never charitable. As Lord Parker commented in *Bowman v Secular Society* (1917),

"A trust for the attainment of political objects has always been held invalid, not because it is illegal . . . but because the court has no means of judging whether a proposed change in the law will or will not be for the public benefit."

As demonstrated in *McGovern v Att-Gen* (1982), if there is an aim to change the law, to promote a particular political party or theory or to seek to change governmental policy either here or abroad it is not charitable. For example, charities dealing with poverty are not allowed to campaign against the social and economic causes of poverty. In *National Anti-Vivisection Society v Inland Revenue Commissioners* (1948), money was given to further the cause of anti-vivisection. The court held that the moral benefit resulting to mankind was outweighed by the detriment that would be suffered by medical research if experiments were not allowed on live animals. The case failed also because it had a political element in that it sought to promote legislation to change the law that allowed vivisection.

3. Exclusively charitable? As with the other heads of charity, the gift must be exclusively charitable. In *McGovern v Att-Gen* (1982), Amnesty International sought charitable status. Although the social benefits of Amnesty's work are readily apparent and look to be caught by the fourth head (*e.g.* promotion of human rights, assisting prisoners of conscience and seeking the abolition of torture and inhumane punishment), it was not exclusively charitable. Its major aims included changing the law and influencing the policies of governments around the world. It was tainted with a political character.

Charities: the future?

In 2003, the government published a number of recommended reforms in "Charities and Not-for-Profits: A Modern Legal Framework". Put simply, it was felt that the four heads of charity did not accurately reflect the range of organisations that should be regarded as charitable in modern times. Accordingly, the Government accepted the need for a new, more flexible, definition focusing on public benefit.

The following list of charitable purposes appear likely to be included in a forthcoming Charities Bill:

  (i) the prevention and relief of poverty;
  (ii) the advancement of education;

  (iii) the advancement of religion;
  (iv) the advancement of health;
   (v) social and community advancement;
  (vi) the advancement of culture, arts and heritage;
 (vii) the advancement of amateur sport;
(viii) the promotion of human rights, conflict resolution and reconciliation;
  (ix) the advancement of environmental protection and improvement;
   (x) the promotion of animal welfare;
  (xi) the provision of social housing;
 (xii) the advancement of science; and,
(xiii) other purposes beneficial to the community.

As to the public benefit tests, there will be no new statutory definition of public benefit. All charities will, however, need to demonstrate that they benefit a sufficiently wide section of the community.

---

13.   THE CY-PRES DOCTRINE

Meaning

A trust can fail for a variety of reasons, *e.g.* it might be illegal, impossible or impracticable to carry out the settlor's wishes. In private trusts, this will give rise to a resulting trust in favour of the settlor or his estate. This is, however, not always so with charitable trusts because the courts have both an inherent jurisdiction and an extended statutory jurisdiction (ss.13 and 14 of the Charities Act 1993) to invoke the cy-pres doctrine. The doctrine allows them to apply the funds to similar charitable bodies or charitable purposes.

Inherent jurisdiction

The court's inherent jurisdiction is limited and can be claimed only where the performance of the trust is impossible or impractical. Unlike the statutory jurisdiction, it does not operate when the trust is cumbersome, inconvenient or uneconomical.

In *Att-Gen v City of London* (1790) the trust included the advancement and propagation of the Christian religion among the infidels of Virginia. It was held that the purpose had become impossible as there were no infidels left in Virginia. Cy-pres was allowed.

A creative use of cy-pres occurred in *Re Lysaght* (1966). The testatrix provided funds to found medical scholarships to be run by the Royal College of Surgeons. One of the terms was that the awards were not to be made to Jews or Roman Catholics. The Royal College refused to accept the gift on these terms so it became impractical to carry out the trust. The court, therefore, deleted the religious discrimination clause.

In *JW Laing Trust* (1984), the court was invited to dispense with the donor's requirement that capital and income had to be distributed no later than 10 years after his death. The dramatic increase in value of the trust fund, however, meant that the named charities could not handle such a colossal cash injection. It was held that the provision could be deleted under the court's inherent jurisdiction because the settlor's demands were of an administrative nature only.

1. Initial failure. Many gifts to specific charities fail because the charity has ceased to exist before the date of the gift. This is called "initial impossibility". In these cases, the trust property can be applied cy-pres under a scheme drawn up by the courts or the Charity Commissioners provided that the settlor had a general charitable intention. The need for a general charitable intention means that, if the gift is solely for a particular purpose, it will fail and leave no room for cy-pres. In *Re Rymer* (1895), there was a specific intention to benefit a seminary for priests that no longer existed. There could be no cy-pres because it was viewed as a gift to a particular body for a particular purpose. A similar stance was adopted in *Re Spence* (1979) where there was initial failure of a gift to a named old people's home that had ceased to exist. As the gift could not be construed as being to the old in the area, there was no general charitable intention. Conversely, a general charitable intention was found in *Biscoe v Jackson* (1887) where money was set aside to finance a soup kitchen and a cottage hospital in Shoreditch. It was not possible to build the hospital, but the money was applied cy-pres because the specified purposes were only two methods of helping the poor of Shoreditch. The charitable intention was general and not specific or limited.

In *Re Harwood* (1936), one gift was made in favour of the Belfast Peace Society and another in favour of the Wisbech Peace Society. The Belfast Peace Society had never existed. The court allowed the application of the gift cy-pres because only a general charitable intention could be attributed to a donor who incorrectly identified the beneficiary of the gift. The other gift could not be applied cy-pres. Accordingly, it is much easier to identify a general charitable intention where a charity had never existed at all.

A named charity may have ceased to function, but may still be continuing in another form. It may, for example, have been amalgamated or reconstituted under different trusts. In *Re Faraker* (1912), a gift to Mrs Bailey's charity, Rotherhithe passed into the hands of a new body that was created by an amalgamation of that charity and several others. The legacy was applied cy-pres for the consolidated charities.

In Re *Finger's Will Trusts* (1972), there was a gift to the National Radium Commission (an unincorporated association) and a gift to the National Council for Maternity and Child Welfare (an incorporated body). When the testatrix died both bodies had ceased to exist (*i.e.* there was initial impossibility). The purposes of the National Radium Commission continued to exist and the gift was held to be a gift to those purposes. It did not matter that the donee no longer existed. The gift to the incorporated body *prima facie* should have failed. It was a gift to that particular body not on trust for its purposes. The court, however, found on the particular facts of the case the testatrix had a paramount charitable intention and so the gift was applied cy-pres.

When a failed charitable gift is one of a number of other charitable gifts in the same document (*e.g.* the same will), the traditional rule is that this association does not make it easier to discern a general charitable intention: *Re Jenkins* (1966). As Buckley J. admitted, "if you meet seven men with black hair and one with red hair you are not entitled to say that there are eight men with black hair." Conversely, in *Re Sattherwaite's Will Trust* (1966) eight animal charities were selected at random from the phone book. One has ceased to exist, but the court was able to infer a general charitable intention.

2. Subsequent failure. In other cases a charity might cease to exist after the property has become vested in the charity. This is known as "subsequent failure". The cy-pres doctrine will apply here irrespective of whether or not there is a general charitable intention. Accordingly, there is no chance of a resulting trust to the donor. In *Re Slevin* (1891), money was dedicated to an orphanage. Although the orphanage was in existence at the testator's death, it had ceased to operate before the money came into its hands. Nevertheless, the money became legally vested in it on the death. This was considered a straightforward case of subsequent failure and the money was applied cy-pres. In *Re King* (1923), a gift was made to provide a stained glass window in a church. On completion of the work, there remained a residue of over £1,000. It was held that this surplus could be applied cy-pres even though there was no general charitable intention shown by the donor.

The time for deciding whether there is an initial failure is at the time of the gift. If the gift is possible at that time, but becomes impossible before it is available for the charity, it still counts as a case of subsequent impossibility. In *Re Wright* (1954), the testatrix died in 1933 leaving her residuary estate to a tenant for life, the remainder to be used to found a house for convalescent and impecunious gentlewomen. By the time the life tenant died in 1942, it was impracticable to found the home. The court found that dedication to charity occurred in 1933 and so the gift could be applied cy-pres without the need of finding any paramount charitable intent.

Statutory jurisdiction: s.13

Section 13 extends the circumstances in which cy-pres is available and intends to modernise the law. It goes beyond impossibility and impracticability and allows cy-pres on the basis of convenience and efficacy. Section 13 prescribes five situations where cy-pres is appropriate:

(i) when the original purposes have been fulfilled or cannot be carried out as intended;

(ii) when the original purposes provide a use for part only of the donated money;

(iii) when the property donated and other property applicable for similar purposes can be more effectively used in conjunction;

(iv) when the original purposes were laid down by reference to an area or by reference to a class of persons which has for any reason since ceased to exist or to be suitable;

(v) where the original purposes, in whole or in part, have been adequately provided for by other means; ceased to be charitable; or ceased to provide a suitable and effective method of using the property donated.

In *Re Lepton's Charity* (1972), a will dated 1715 directed that £3 per annum was to be paid to the local minister and any surplus income to the poor. By 1970, the trust income had risen from £5 to £800. The court increased the minister's stipend to £100 per annum. Modern conditions entailed that £3 was not in keeping with the spirit of the gift.

In *Varsani v Jesani* (1998), the court enabled a gift to be divided between two conflicting groups of a Hindu sect. The charity had divided into two factions and it became impossible to achieve the original purposes that had been envisaged. The property (a temple) was not, therefore, being used in accordance with the spirit of the gift.

In *Peggs v Lamb* (1994), a cy-pres scheme was authorised in circumstances where a charitable purpose, which was originally for the benefit of the freemen of a borough, was enlarged to cover the inhabitants of the borough as a whole. This was because those who would qualify as freemen had declined in numbers to 15 and the income to be distributed had risen to £559,000 per annum.

Statutory jurisdiction: s.14

The idea underlying s.14 of the Charities Act 1993 is that, where money is donated to charity through collecting boxes, lotteries, competitions and so forth, cy-pres might operate to prevent a resulting trust arising.

The provision applies only to initial failure and only in circumstances where the donor has disclaimed or cannot be identified or found. There is a presumption, in relation to cash collections and fund-raising events, that the donors are unidentifiable. In such cases, the money can be applied cy-pres regardless of whether there is evidence of general charitable intention. The aim is to prevent the charity having to track down individual donors.

14. APPOINTMENT, RETIREMENT AND REMOVAL OF TRUSTEES

Capacity and number

Generally any person who has the capacity to hold property can be a trustee. A minor cannot be appointed a trustee nor can he hold a legal estate in *land*: s.20 of the Law of Property Act 1925. A minor can, however be a trustee of *personal property* held on an implied trust. In *Re Vinogradoff* (1935), a grandmother put War Loan stock into the names of herself and her granddaughter. The granddaughter was only four years old. It was held that, as there was no presumption of advancement in the child's favour, she became a trustee holding the property on a resulting trust for her grandmother. Infancy is, moreover, one of the grounds for removing a trustee and appointing another under s.36(1) of the Trustee Act 1925.

A corporation can be a trustee. Some corporations are known as trust corporations. These include the Public Trustee, the Treasury Solicitor, the Official Solicitor, certain charitable or public corporations and those corporations entitled to act as custodian trustees under the Public Trustee Act 1906.

In a trust or settlement of *land*, the maximum permitted number of trustees is four. The minimum number is one trustee. In order to ensure that trust interests are overreached (*i.e.* taken free of) by a purchaser, however, the purchase money must be paid to at least two trustees or a trust corporation. Hence, if there is a sole trustee of land, the prospective purchaser should require that an additional trustee be appointed. The trustees of land must always hold the legal title as joint tenants. This means that, if one dies, the surviving trustees continue until only one remains alive. As regards a trust of *personal* property, there is no limit on the number of trustees who can be appointed.

Appointment of trustees

There is a general equitable principle that "equity does not want for a trustee". This means that a trust will not fail if, for example, the appointed trustees refuse to act or have ceased to exist. If necessary, the Public Trustee will act in the capacity of trustee. An exception to this rule arises when the trust is made conditional upon certain people acting as trustees: *Hill v Royal College of Surgeons* (1966).

As regards *initial trustees*, they are generally appointed in the will or settlement. The settlor chooses who he wishes to be trustee. When one of the initial trustees dies, the property vests in the survivor(s). When the last survivor dies, the property vests in his personal representatives, subject to the trust: s.18 of the Trustee Act 1925.

As to the appointment of *subsequent trustees*, the trust terms or statute may give some individuals the power to appoint new trustees:

(i) Unless there is an express power for him to do so, the settlor cannot appoint new trustees once the trust has been properly constituted.

(ii) As to the beneficiaries, s.19 of the Trusts of Land and Appointment of Trustees Act 1996 gives them a power to give a written direction to a trustee or trustees for the time being, including anyone being directed to retire at the same time, to appoint as a trustee or trustees the person or persons specified in the direction. If there are no trustees, the direction has to be given to the personal representative of the last person who was a trustee. The beneficiaries must be of full age and capacity and together absolutely entitled to the trust property. This power can be excluded in the trust instrument, for example, when a power to appoint trustees is vested in someone nominated for the purpose in the trust instrument. Hence, it only applies where the trust instrument makes no provision for the appointment of new trustees.

(iii) In other cases, trustees may be appointed under the auspices of s.36 of the Trustee Act 1925. If there is a conflict between the trust instrument and the s.36 power, the statutory power prevails.

(iv) Where a trustee is incapable by reason of mental disorder, and there is no one able and willing to exercise the s.36 power, s.20 of the Trusts of Land and Appointment of Trustees Act 1996 enables the beneficiaries to direct his replacement.

Appointment under s.36 of the Trustee Act 1925

Although the trust instrument may confer an express power of appointment of trustees, reliance is placed (usually by the settlor or trustees) on the wide statutory power as set out in s.36 of the

Trustee Act 1925. The trust instrument, however, will usually nominate those who may exercise the statutory power.

Unless there is a contrary provision in the trust instrument, s.36 provides that *a replacement trustee* may be appointed when a trustee:

(i) has died (this includes a person appointed in a will who dies before the testator); or,

(ii) has remained outside the UK for a continuous period exceeding 12 months. This ground is often expressly excluded where for tax reasons all the trust property is outside the UK; or,

(iii) seeks to retire from the trust; or,

(iv) refuses to act or disclaims the role before accepting office; or,

(v) is unfit to act (*e.g.* where he has become bankrupt); or,

(vi) is incapable of acting. This includes physical and mental illness, old age and, in the case of a corporation, dissolution; or,

(vii) is an infant; or,

(viii) has been removed under a power in the trust instrument.

The aim of s.36 is to ensure that there will be someone who has the ability to appoint a new trustee if necessary. To this end, s.36 provides that, subject to someone having been nominated in the trust instrument, an appointment should be made by:

(i) the persons nominated in the trust instrument; or, failing such a person:

(ii) all the beneficiaries who are of full age and capacity and together absolutely entitled to the trust property; or, failing such appointment:

(iii) the surviving or continuing trustees; or, if no trustees are living:

(iv) the personal representatives of the last surviving or continuing trustee. This, of course, has no application where it is an *additional* trustee that is being appointed; or, on the failure of all of the above:

(v) the court under s.41 of the Trustee Act 1925.

Where a trustee is replaced, anyone can be appointed a new trustee including the appointer himself. He cannot, however, appoint himself when an *additional* trustee is being appointed under s.36(6).

Appointment by the court

Under s.41 of the Trustee Act 1925, the court has a wide power to appoint new trustees "either in substitution for or in addition to any existing trustee or trustees, or although there is no existing trustee". In particular the court may appoint a new trustee where any existing trustee is mentally unfit to act, or is a bankrupt, or being a corporation, is in liquidation or has been dissolved. An order can be made on the application of either a trustee or beneficiary: s.58.

The court will not appoint a person excluded from being a trustee under s.36(1) (*e.g.* a person under a mental disability or living abroad) and it will be reluctant to appoint a beneficiary because of a possible conflict in interest. In *Re Tempest* (1866), Turner L.J. stated that the court should have regard to the wishes of the person by whom the trust was created, the interests (even if conflicting) of all the beneficiaries and the efficient administration of the trust.

Under the Judicial Trustee Act 1896, either the settlor, a trustee, or a beneficiary can make an application for the appointment of a trustee by the court. The court can appoint any fit person nominated in the application or an official of the court, to act solely or jointly with other trustees. A Judicial Trustee is a paid officer of the court and subject to its control and supervision.

Under the Public Trustee Act 1906, on an application by a trustee or beneficiary the court has power to appoint the Public Trustee as a new or additional trustee.

Vesting of trust property

On their appointment, the trust property has to become vested in the new trustees. Section 40 of the Trustee Act 1925 provides that, where the trustee is appointed by deed, a "vesting declaration" in the deed will operate to vest the property in the new trustees. Such a declaration may be implied, subject to any provision in the deed to the contrary. There is, therefore, no need for an express conveyance or assignment.

Section 40 does not apply to:

(i) land mortgaged to secure money subject to a trust. This keeps the trusts off the title. Trustees who lend money on mortgage do not disclose the existence of the trust. On the appointment of new trustees there must be a separate transfer of the mortgage. The borrower will thus know to whom to repay the money without inspecting the trust instrument and deeds of appointment;

(ii) land held under a lease which contains a covenant against assignment without consent unless the consent has been obtained before the execution of the deed. This prevents the appointment causing an inadvertent breach of covenant against assignment;

(iii) stocks and shares. This recognises that the legal title to shares can only be effected by registration with the relevant company.

Terminating trusteeship

1. Disclaimer. A person is not bound to accept the onerous duties of a trustee just because he is named in a trust instrument or because he has previously agreed to be a trustee. He must, however, disclaim before he has done any act indicating acceptance. He cannot disclaim part only of the trust: *Re Lord Fullertons Contract* (1896). When disclaiming a trust it is advisable, albeit not essential, to do so by deed. If the trustee disclaiming is the sole trustee, the trust property will result to the settlor or his personal representatives upon trust. If there are other trustees the property will remain with them.

2. Retirement. A trustee may retire under s.36(1) of the Trustee Act 1925 on being replaced by someone else. Under s.39, a trustee may retire by deed from the trust provided that either a trust corporation or at least two trustees will be left after his retirement or his co-trustees (and the person, if any, entitled to appoint new trustees) consent by deed. Where the Public Trustee has been appointed a co-trustee can retire without these conditions being fulfilled.

The deed of retirement will normally contain a declaration by the retiring trustee vesting the property in the continuing trustees. A declaration will be implied unless there is a contrary intention.

Mortgages, leases with a covenant against assignment, and stocks and shares will have to be transferred separately as on appointment: s.40(2),(3) of the Trustee Act 1925.

3. Removal. A trustee can be removed on the grounds set out in s.36(1) (see above). The court also has an inherent jurisdiction to remove a trustee. In *Letterstedt v Broers* (1884), a beneficiary made several allegations of misconduct against the trustees and asked for their removal. He succeeded. It was held that the duty of the court was to ensure the proper execution of the trust. Even if the facts are disputed, or the trustees can disprove the allegations, they may be removed if there is disharmony. The welfare of the beneficiary is paramount.

On the other hand the court can consider the expense to the trust of a change of trustees and decide against removal even where there has been a minor breach of trust: *Re Wrightson* (1908). A trustee who sets up a rival business might not be in breach of trust, but the conflict of interest would be a ground for his removal: *Moore v M'Glynn* (1896).

4. *Direction by beneficiary to retire.* The Trusts of Land and Appointment of Trustees Act 1996 provides that beneficiaries (who are unanimous, of full age and capacity and between them entitled to the whole beneficial interest) may direct the retirement of a trustee. The conditions for the compulsory pensioning off of a trustee are:

(i) a written direction must be given to him;
(ii) reasonable arrangements must be made for the protection of any rights of his in connection with the trust;
(iii) on his retirement there must remain a trust corporation or at least two trustees;
(iv) a new trustee must be appointed on his retirement or, if no such appointment is to be made, the continuing trustees must consent by deed to his retirement;
(v) the retiring trustee must execute a deed of discharge (he has the ability to defer the deed until reasonable arrangements for his protection have been made); and
(vi) the retiring and continuing trustees and any new trustee must do anything necessary to vest the trust property in the continuing and new trustees.

A trustee who is directed to retire may have rights in respect of the trust property. He might have rights of reimbursement or indemnity for expenses incurred in relation to the trust and he may need to take action to ensure that he can enforce those rights. He may also need to guard himself against taxation liabilities for which he could be held responsible after his retirement or he may have incurred contractual liabilities to third parties in dealing with the trust property. The 1996 Act, therefore, provides that he shall only be under an obligation to execute a deed of retirement after reasonable arrangements have been made for the protection of any rights of his in connection with the trust.

---

15.   TRUSTEE'S DUTIES

The duties of a trustee are extremely onerous. They have to be carried out with the utmost diligence. If not, the trustee will be liable for breach of trust. Some duties arise automatically from the relationship between trustee and beneficiary while others are imposed and regulated by statute. Paramount to a trustee's functions is the fiduciary duty that is imposed by equity. This places an obligation of loyalty and faithfulness upon the shoulders of a trustee. The fiduciary duty entails that, put simply, the trustee must act in utmost good faith.

Duties on appointment

The trustees are under a duty to call in the trust property. Accordingly, if part of the property is a loan due for repayment, this should be called in. If it becomes statute-barred under the Limitation Act 1980, the trustees are personally liable. The only defence would be if they could show that they have a well-founded belief that any enforcement action would be pointless: *Re Brogden* (1888).

The trust property ought to be placed in the joint control of all the trustees. In *Lewis v Nobbs* (1878), the trust property included bearer bonds half of which were in the sole control of each trustee. When one of the trustees went off with the half in his custody, the other trustee was held liable.

Under the Trustee Act 2002, in relation to so-called "bearer securities" (*i.e.* securities which are not registered in the name of anyone) the trustees must appoint a custodian of any such security unless exempted by the trust instrument or by statutory provision. These securities cannot be placed in the names of the trustees.

The trustees should investigate any previous breaches of trust. Otherwise, the trustees may be personally liable for any loss that arose from a lack of inquiry.

General fiduciary duties

1. *Duty not to make a profit.* The trustee may not make an unauthorised profit from his position as trustee. He must not put himself in a position where his duty to the trust and his own personal interest may conflict. In *Keech v Sandford* (1726), a trustee of a lease applied for its renewal for the benefit of an infant beneficiary. It was refused, but the landlord agreed to renew the lease in the trustee's own favour. There was no question of fraud, but it was concluded that the trustee held the lease on trust for the infant. The reason was that there would be less incentive on the trustee to press for a renewal for the trust if he knew that he would benefit by a refusal.

The rule in *Keech v Sandford*, however, applies only when a trustee or some other fiduciary obtains the benefit. In *Re Biss* (1903), a yearly tenant of a shop died intestate and a renewal was refused to his widow. Although one of their children subsequently obtained a renewal, he was entitled to keep the lease for himself. No fiduciary duty was owed to the estate.

2. *Purchase of the trust estate.* However fair the transaction, the purchase of trust property by a trustee is voidable by any beneficiary. The rule is sometimes referred to as the "self-dealing rule": *Tito v Waddell (No.2)* (1977). The beneficiaries' ability to set aside the transaction applies even if the property was bought at a public auction: *Ex p. Lacey* (1802). The rule has been held not to apply fully to a bona fide sale to a relative. Similarly, it will not usually extend to a purchase by a company in which the trustee has shares. This gives way, however, when the trustee is a majority shareholder or controls the company: *Farrars v Farrars Ltd* (1888).

If a trustee retires in order to purchase trust property, the sale remains voidable. This intention will be presumed where the sale follows closely after retirement. In *Re Boles and British Land Co's Contract* (1902), a sale was not set aside where the trustee had retired 12 years before he purchased the property. If a trustee obtains an option to purchase, the court is likely to set it aside as the trustee could exercise his option when prices are low. In *Wright v Morgan* (1926), an option was avoided even though an independent valuer had fixed the price. An option was, however, upheld in *Re Mulholland's Will Trusts* (1949). There the option was granted to a bank by a testator before the bank took up the trusteeship on his death.

If expressly authorised to do so by the trust instrument or by the court, the trustee is permitted to purchase the trust property. For example, s.68 of the Settled Land Act 1925 enables the tenant for life to purchase trust property.

The self-dealing rule is not simply confined to situations where the trustee is both vendor and purchaser. In *Re Thompson's Settlement* (1986), a trustee concurred in a transaction that would not otherwise have been entered. The transferee was a company of which the trustee was a managing director and in which his family had a majority shareholding. The transfer was voidable.

3. *Buying out the beneficiary.* In this scenario, the trustee is not buying from himself, there is an initial presumption of validity. This rule is sometimes referred to as the "fair-dealing rule". In *Morse v Royal* (1806), a middle-aged ex-army officer sold his interest to the trustee. There was no concealment or deceit by the trustee. When the property went up in price the beneficiary, who had pressed the trustee to buy the property, regretted the sale and sought to have it set aside. He failed.

4. *Remunerative employment.* A trustee must not use his position in order to obtain paid employment. In *Williams v Barton* (1927), a stockbroker trustee had to hand over to the trust the commission he earned on valuation by his firm of the trust assets.

Often a trustee will obtain remuneration as a director of a company. If the directorship was acquired because of his position as a trustee, he will be accountable to the trust: *Re Macadam* (1946). This is not so, however, if the trustees were directors before they became trustees (*Re Dover Coalfield Extension Ltd* (1908)) or if the trustees were appointed directors without any reliance on the trust votes (*Re Gee* (1948)). The will or settlement may, moreover, authorise the trustee to keep any remuneration: *Re Llewellin's Will Trusts* (1949).

Similar principles apply to such characters as bankers, company directors and business partners. They are accountable for any profits they make because of their position. In *Boardman v Phipps* (1967), a solicitor (Mr Boardman) administered a business in which the trust had an interest and made large profits both for the trust and himself. Although he had acted bona fide throughout, he was held accountable for his personal gains subject to a liberal allowance for his expertise and hard work. Mr Boardman had only been able to make the profit because of the confidential information he had received while administering the trust.

5. Payment for acting as trustee. One of the consequences of the rule that a trustee must not make a profit from his trust is that a trustee cannot charge for his time and trouble: *Barrett v Hartley* (1866). Even a solicitor trustee cannot charge for anything other than his out-of-pocket expenses. There are, however, exceptions to this rule:

  (i) if all the beneficiaries are *sui juris*, and there is no possibility of undue influence, they can agree to the trustee being paid;

  (ii) the court has a statutory jurisdiction to authorise payment where it appoints a corporation to be a trustee: s.42 of the Trustee Act 1925;

  (iii) a Judicial Trustee may be paid out of trust property: s.1(5) of the Judicial Trustees Act 1896;

  (iv) the Public Trustee or a custodian trustee can charge under the Public Trustee Act 1906;

  (v) the court has an inherent jurisdiction to allow a trustee to be paid where there is no charging clause in the trust instrument. Alternatively, it can vary or increase the amount that can be charged when there is a charging clause. The services of the trustee must, however, be regarded as being of exceptional benefit to the trust. In *Re Duke of Norfolk's Settlement* (1981), a trust corporation accepted the administration of the trust for a low annual fee. As trustee, it subsequently became involved in an extensive redevelopment project and was allowed an increase in remuneration because the duties became unexpectedly onerous;

  (vi) solicitor-trustees' costs of litigation are the subject of special treatment. According to the rule in *Cradock v Piper* (1850), a solicitor-trustee is entitled to profit costs in litigation where he acts as solicitor for himself and a co-trustee in relation to the trust. This is provided that the costs are no more than they would have been had he acted for the co-trustee alone. A solicitor-trustee cannot employ his firm to do non-litigious work;

(vii) the trust instrument may authorise the remuneration of the trustee. Many professional trustees, of course, would not undertake the trusteeship without the presence of an express charging clause. In such cases, s.28(2) of the Trustee Act 2000 entitles a trustee acting in a professional capacity to charge ". . . in respect of services even if they are services which are capable of being provided for by a lay trustee." Previously, the trustee could charge only for the work that required his professional skills: *Re Gee* (1948);

(viii) where there is no entitlement to remuneration given by the trust instrument or by another statutory provision, s.29 of the Trustee Act 2000 offers additional entitlements. First, a trustee that is a trust corporation is entitled to "reasonable remuneration". Secondly, a trustee who acts in a "professional capacity" is also entitled to "reasonable remuneration" provided that each of the other trustees agree in writing. Section 29, therefore, does not apply if there is a sole trustee.

6. *Recovery of out of pocket expenses.* A trustee is entitled to be reimbursed for out of pocket expenses such as insurance premiums, fees paid to brokers and money spent on repairs. Section 31(1) of the Trustee Act 2000 provides that a trustee has a right to recover "expenses properly incurred by him when acting on the behalf of the trust".

A trustee will also be allowed his litigation costs if the court grants leave to sue or defend. In other cases, the trustee will obtain costs only if the action was properly brought or defended for the benefit of the trust estate: *Holding & Management Ltd v Property Holding & Investment Trusts plc* (1990).

7. *Competitive business.* If the trust contains a business as part of its assets then the trustee should not compete. In *Re Thompson* (1930), the trust property included a yacht broker's business. A trustee wanted to set up a similar business in the same locality. The court issued an injunction restraining the trustee because his plans would have taken trade away from the trust business.

8. *Duty to keep accounts and provide information.* Trustees must keep clear and accurate accounts and produce them to any beneficiary when required. A beneficiary is entitled to all reasonable information about the administration of the trust. When a beneficiary reaches 18 years of age, he should be informed of his interest under the trust.

Beneficiaries are entitled to see all trust documents and title deeds: *O'Rourke v Darbishire* (1920). Trustees are not, however, bound to give reasons why they have exercised their discretion in a particular way. Hence, they are not bound to disclose documents, such as trust minutes, which contain this confidential information: *Re Londonderry's Settlement* (1965). A disgruntled beneficiary could, however, bring legal proceedings alleging bad faith, and the confidential documents would then be made available on discovery.

Section 22(4) of the Trustee Act 1925 gives the trustees an absolute discretion to have the accounts audited, but no more than once in every three years unless there are special circumstances.

Investment and the Trustee Act 2000

1. *Standard of care.* The standard of care expected of a trustee has been defined in s.1 of the Trustee Act 2000. This provides that the trustee must exercise such care and skill as is reasonable in the circumstances having regard:

(i) to any special knowledge or experience that he has or holds himself out as having, and

(ii) if he acts as trustee in the course of a business or profession, to any special knowledge or experience that it is reasonable to expect of a person acting in the course of that business or profession.

It was hoped that the s.1 duty would be higher than that previously imposed at common law. It extends to cover the power of investment, the acquisition of land, the entering into arrangements to appoint agents and nominees, the exercise of powers of compromise and insurance and the valuation of trust property. Nevertheless, the custody and management of trust property and defending proceedings on behalf of the trust are not specifically mentioned and might not, therefore, be subject to the statutory duty of care.

2. *Duty of investment.* Unless the trust instrument contains an express investment clause, the duty to invest is regulated by the Trustee Act 2000. This duty is designed to ensure that the trustees treat income and capital beneficiaries in an impartial manner. This might be described as a duty to act fairly between all beneficiaries. As Hoffmann J. admitted,

> "The trustees must act fairly in making investment decisions which may have different consequences for different classes of beneficiaries" (*Nestle' v National Westminster Bank plc* (1988)).

It is also intended to minimise risk while the trustees achieve a reasonable return on the capital invested.

Section 3 offers the trustee a general power of investment and authorises ". . . any kind of investment that he could make if he were absolutely entitled to the assets of the trust". The general duty of care set out in s.1 (above) applies to the making of investments. An investment for these purposes requires an anticipation of profit or income (*e.g.* granting a mortgage on terms that it will be repaid with interest). This rids the law of the authorised categorisations previously set out in the (now repealed) Trustee Investments Act 1961.

Section 8 gives the trustee the general power to acquire land whether or not it is designed to generate a rental income. It might be used, for example, to provide a home for a beneficiary.

Section 4 requires the trustees when making an investment to have regard to the suitability of particular investments and the need for diversification. These are described as the "standard investment criteria". As the trustees are required to add diversity to their investment portfolio, they have to be judged on overall performance and not the failure or success of a particular investment: *Nestle v National Westminster Bank Plc* (1988). Of course, the trustees must carry out periodic reviews of their investment portfolio and, if necessary, vary the investments.

Section 5 requires the trustees to obtain and consider investment advice from a suitable source. The source could be an expert trustee or an outside adviser. This rule gives way when it would be reasonable to proceed without such advice (*e.g.* if the investment is small). Trustees are not obliged to follow the advice received, but if they decline to do so they run the risk of being liable for any resultant loss.

Investment: the prudent man test

The trustees must invest the trust property wisely acting as a prudent man making investments "for the benefit of other people for whom he felt morally bound to provide"(*Learoyd v Whiteley* (1887)). Trustees must obtain the best rate of return available coupled with diversification of risks even where it is against the political, social or moral views of some of the beneficiaries (*Cowan v Scargill* (1984)).

Although charitable trustees can exclude certain investments (*e.g.* in armaments), they cannot pursue a complete policy of ethical investment as this would be detrimental to value of the trust fund (*Harries v Church Commissioners* (1992)).

In *Re Whiteley* (1886), a trustee was held to account for imprudently investing £3,000 upon the mortgage of a brick-works. The land did not offer sufficient security. When the business failed, the loan could not be recouped. In *Bartlett v Barclays Bank* (1980), the trust company (Barclays) invested in a property company who embarked upon a series of unwise property speculations. The Bank, as trustee, stood by and did nothing. It was held that the Bank was liable for the losses incurred.

As shown, s.1 of the Trustee Act 2000 imposes a higher standard of care upon those who claim a specialism or expertise. Hence, a trust company with specialist staff will be judged on a different level to an unpaid, family trustee: see *Bartlett v Barclays Bank* (1980).

Trustees and trusts of land

The Trusts of Land and Appointment of Trustees Act 1996 applies to trusts of land and gives the trustees the powers of absolute owners. Nevertheless, the Act specifically gives certain beneficiaries the right to occupy trust land. This right may, however, be restricted or excluded in certain circumstances.

It is only beneficiaries entitled to an interest in possession in the land that have a right to occupy. This ensures that benefici-aries of pension schemes will not qualify to occupy the land. Those with a purely monetary interest, such an annuitants, are excluded. Excluded also are those with a future or contingent interest.

The purposes of the trust must include making the land available for the occupation of the particular beneficiary. Alter-natively, the land must be held by the trustees so as to be available for occupation. It does not have to be acquired specifically for that purpose. A house might have been acquired for resale, but subsequently the trustees might decide not to sell the property but to allow the beneficiary to reside there.

Although a beneficiary might have a *prima facie* right to occupy, the claim will fail if the land is unavailable or unsuitable for occupation. An example of premises being unsuitable would be where a farm became available, but the beneficiary had no farming experience or expertise.

Where two or more beneficiaries have a right to occupy, the trustees have power to regulate the occupation. They may restrict or exclude the right of one or more to occupy the property. The trustees cannot, however, exclude the rights of occupation of all the beneficiaries. In exercising their power to exclude or restrict any beneficiary's right to occupancy, the trustees must not act unreasonably. The trustees may also impose conditions on any other beneficiary to make payments to an excluded beneficiary by way of compensation.

Where a beneficiary or beneficiaries have a right to occupy, the trustees may, from time to time, impose reasonable conditions. These conditions are not only for protecting the interests of those with competing rights, but also the interests of those beneficiaries who do not have a right to occupy. Conditions imposed by the trustees may include an obligation to pay outgoings and rent in respect of the land and to assume any other obligation in respect of the land or to an activity carried out thereon.

When exercising their power to exclude or restrict the right to occupy or to impose conditions, the trustees must take into account, amongst other things:

(i) the intentions of those who created the trust;
(ii) the purpose for which the land is held; and
(iii) the circumstances and wishes of each of the beneficiaries who has a right or whose right to occupy the land has been excluded or restricted.

A person who is already in occupation is offered some protection. The trustees may not, in exercising their powers to exclude or restrict occupation, prevent a person either directly or indirectly from continuing in occupation unless that person consents or the court gives approval. In deciding whether to give approval, the court has to take on board the intentions of the person who created the trust, the purpose for which the land is held and the circumstances and wishes of the beneficiaries who are otherwise entitled to occupy the land.

16. POWERS OF MAINTENANCE, ADVANCEMENT AND THE APPOINTMENT OF AGENTS

As well as labouring under the duties imposed by the trust instrument, the common law and statute (see Ch.15), the trustees will have a variety of powers (or discretions). Some of these powers will concern how the trustees may deal with the trust property while others may focus upon how the trustees deal with the beneficiaries. A number of powers are conferred by statute (including the power to sell, partition and insure the trust property: Pts I and II of the Trustee Act 1925) whereas others will be stated expressly in the trust instrument. For the purposes of this chapter, however, only the powers of maintenance, advancement will be considered.

In the exercise of a power the trustees must be unanimous unless there is a provision in the trust instrument to the contrary. The trustees' powers are not, however, mandatory and are merely permissive. They authorise what would otherwise be a breach of trust. The issue as to whether or not to exercise a power is entirely at the discretion of the trustees. The powers are, however, fiduciary in nature. This entails that the trustees are under a duty to consider whether to exercise them. Absent bad faith, if they decide not to exercise their discretion there is nothing that can be done. If the trustees are unsure as to the scope of an express power (or, indeed, a statutory power), it is open for them to apply to the court for directions.

Maintenance

Maintenance is to do with the trustees using trust income to provide for the maintenance or benefit of a minor beneficiary. The trustees' power to do so may arise from the trust instrument or under statute.

1. *Express power.* At common law, there is no general power that allows trustees to divert trust money to provide for the welfare and education of an infant beneficiary. If the trust instrument expressly gives the trustees a discretionary power to apply income for maintenance purposes, the trustees must honestly decide whether to exercise their power. The trustees, however, cannot delegate to someone else a discretionary power that is given to them personally: *Re Greenslade* (1915). Similarly, they cannot give the whole fund to a parent without exercising their discretion at all: *Wilson v Turner* (1883).

2. Statutory power. The statutory power of maintenance is to be found in s.31 of the Trustee Act 1925. This statutory provision does not apply in the face of a contrary intention shown by the settlor: *Re Erskine* (1971). When it does operate, the trustees are entitled to pay, to the parent or guardian of a pre-18-year-old, the whole or part of the income of the property for his maintenance, benefit or education.

Upon reaching 18 years, and if the beneficiary's interest has still not vested, the trustees must (unless there is a direction in the trust instrument to the contrary) pay the whole of the income to the beneficiary. In *Re McGeorge* (1963), the testator bequeathed land to his daughter. The bequest was not to take effect until after the wife's death. The 21-year-old daughter claimed the income. The court held that she was not entitled to maintenance from the income because the gift was deferred. This deferral indicated a contrary intention.

The trustees may only maintain a minor where there is income to which the minor has a right. As demonstrated in *Re Vestey* (1950), a beneficiary under a discretionary trust is not entitled to income and, hence, there is no statutory power to maintain. This entails that the minor's interest (whether "vested" or "contingent") must carry with it an entitlement to the interim income.

A vested interest usually carries with it the right to income. For example, a trust that is contingent upon X reaching the age of 18 will vest when X reaches 18 years. In the intervening period, the beneficiary has a contingent interest. Such a beneficiary will be entitled to income only if the property that is the subject matter of the trust carries the intermediate income.

Unfortunately, it is not always clear whether or not a *contingent interest* brings with it a right to income. The general rule is that all *testamentary* gifts carry the intermediate income, except for deferred residuary gifts and contingent pecuniary legacies: s.175 of the Law of Property Act 1925. Furthermore, in three special cases contingent pecuniary legacies will carry the intermediate income:

(i) where the legacy was given to a minor by his father or some person *in loco parentis*, the contingency is reaching 18, and there is no other fund available for maintenance: s. 31(3) Trustee Act 1925;

(ii) where the testator has shown an intention that the beneficiary should be maintained. In *Re Churchill* (1909), the testatrix gave a pecuniary legacy to her nephew. She directed her trustees to pay money towards the advancement of him in life "or otherwise for his benefit". The court held it carried the intermediate income and so maintenance was available;

(iii) where the testator sets aside a special fund for the legatee, but makes it contingent. For example, a gift of £10,000 to Bella on reaching 18 years of age.

As to *class gifts*, where property is given to a class contingently on attaining 18 years of age, the vesting of one person's share does not prevent the trustees from applying the income from the presumptive shares of the others for their maintenance.

In relation to *accumulation*, if there is an express direction to accumulate income until a certain age, this may indicate that the testator does not want the statutory power of maintenance to apply. Otherwise, and if necessary, the trustees can apply the accumulations for the benefit of any infant beneficiary as if they were income from the current year. Section 31(2) of the Trustee Act 1925 provides that all the income arising during infancy that is not distributed should be accumulated and invested. The beneficiary is entitled to such surplus funds on reaching his majority (or earlier marriage) if either he is then entitled to the capital or during his minority he had a vested interest in the income: s.31(2).

The making of maintenance payments is in the sole discretion of the trustees. By virtue of s.31(1), the payments must be reasonable and the trustees should consider the age of the minor, his requirements and all the circumstances of the case including what other income is available.

Advancement

The power of advancement concerns the possibility of the trustees allowing part of the trust capital to be paid to or used for the benefit of a beneficiary prior to his interest becoming vested.

1. *Express power.* An express power to apply capital (as distinct from income as in maintenance) for the advancement or benefit of a minor or contingent beneficiary is sometimes given in a trust instrument. Advancement concerns the making of some permanent provision for a beneficiary (*e.g.* buying a house for him to set up as medical practitioner: *Re Williams Will Trusts* (1953)).

"Benefit" is given a wide meaning and would, for example, cover the payment of the beneficiary's debts. In *Re Clores Settlement Trusts* (1966), as part of a tax-saving scheme and in order to fulfil the moral obligations of the wealthy beneficiary, capital was applied by making donations to charities. It was considered to be of sufficient benefit to the beneficiary.

Whatever the terms of the power the trustees must exercise their discretion in making the advance and make sure that the purpose of the advance is really carried out. In *Re Pauling's Settlement Trust* (1964), the trustees advanced capital sums to child beneficiaries from their presumptive share. Although nominally for the benefit of the children, the capital was really used to maintain the luxurious lifestyle of their parents. Subsequently the children succeeded in suing the trustees for breach of trust in making improper advances.

2. Statutory power.   Unless there is a contrary intention, every trust now has a statutory power to pay capital for the advancement or benefit of any person entitled to the capital, or any share thereof, even if there is a possibility that the beneficiary's interest may be defeated: s.32 of the Trustee Act 1925. This section is restricted to trust property that is personalty. Where the beneficiary wants to buy trust land, however, it has been held that (rather than give him the money so that he could buy the land) the property could be conveyed direct: *Re Collard's Will Trusts* (1961).

As well as being limited to personal property, the other limitations of the statutory power of advancement are:

(i)   the capital advanced must not exceed half the beneficiary's vested or presumptive share;

(ii)   when the beneficiary's interest vests, any advances must be brought into account in calculating his share; and

(iii)   the advance must not prejudice the prior life, or other interest of any person (*e.g.* a life tenant) unless he is *sui juris* and gives his written consent.

The trustees can apply the money "in such manner as they may, in their absolute discretion, think fit". Benefit, as in express

powers of advancement, is given a wide meaning. "It means
any use of the money which will improve the material situation
of the beneficiary" (*per* Viscount Radcliffe in *Pilkington v Inland
Revenue Commissioners* (1964)). In *Pilkington,* the trustees suggested that, in order to save tax, an advance be made to a young
beneficiary and that the advance should be resettled on new
trusts. It was held that such an exercise was within the statutory
power and that it did not matter that incidentally the family of
the beneficiary might benefit.

The appointment of agents

The traditional rule is that a trustee cannot delegate his trust
powers and duties and this is known as the duty of personal
service: *Speight v Gaunt* (1883). The rule reflects the fact that the
trustee is likely to have been chosen for his personal qualities
and wisdom. Nevertheless, trustees have always been able to
delegate where special skills are required. For example, a
stockbroker could be employed to buy and sell shares and a
solicitor to undertake conveyancing work. The power to appoint
agents is now governed by the Trustee Act 2000. Under s.11,
there is a general power that allows trustees to delegate their
functions to an agent (including one of themselves, but not a
beneficiary).

The 2000 Act, however, makes some functions incapable of
delegation. These are:

  (i) any function concerning whether or in what manner the
      assets of the trust should be distributed;
 (ii) the power to decide whether the payment of fees should
      be made out of capital or income;
(iii) any power to appoint a new trustee;
(iv) any power capable of delegation under the trust instru-
      ment or another statutory provision.

As regards a charitable trust, a different approach is adopted.
The general rule is that there can be no delegation except as
provided for by in s.11(3). This allows the delegation of:

  (i) purely ministerial functions in carrying out decisions
      already made;
 (ii) any function relating to the investment of assets subject to
      the trust;

(iii) any function relating to the raising of funds for the trust (otherwise than by means of profits of a trade carried on by the charity as an integral part of its purpose).

When an agent is authorised to exercise a function that is subject to specific duties (*e.g.* having regard to the standard investment criteria) then the agent will usually be subject to those duties. The duty to consult beneficiaries under the Trusts of Land and Appointment of Trustees Act 1996 does not, however, apply to agents.

Section 15 contains special provisions that apply to agents who are to exercise asset management functions (*e.g.* the investment, management and buying and selling of trust property). The agreement with the agent must be put in written form. It must, moreover, oblige the agent to comply with a pre-prepared statement of the trustees which offers guidance as to how the agent should carry out his work in the best interests of the trust.

Appointment of nominees and custodians

Modern practice is that investment securities are usually held in the name of nominees in order to cater for a quick sale (*i.e.* for administrative convenience). A custodian is someone who agrees to take safe custody of trust assets or documents. This common practice is again central to modern investment business. There is, however, no intention that either character becomes a trustee. Sections 16–19 of the Trustee Act 2000 Act facilitate the appointment of nominees and custodians. Trustees can make such an appointment in three cases:

(i) a power to appoint a nominee in relation to assets of the trust as the trustees determine and to take such steps as are necessary to secure that those assets are vested in him;

(ii) a power to appoint a custodian in relation to such assets as they determine;

(iii) where the trust property includes bearer securities, a duty to appoint a custodian of those securities.

The appointment must be put into written form and the appointee must either be a professional nominee/custodian, a company controlled by the trustees or a firm of solicitors.

Liability for agents

Section 23(1) of the Trustee Act 2000 provides that a trustee is not liable for any act or default of an agent, nominee or custodian. This rule gives way when the trustee has failed to comply with his statutory duty of care (see Ch.15) when entering into arrangements with such persons or by failing to keep those arrangements under review.

Delegation under the Trusts of Land and Appointment of Trustees Act 1996

Section 9 of the Trusts of Land and Appointment of Trustees Act 1996 expressly enables trustees of a trust of land collectively to delegate their powers, including the power of sale, to beneficiaries of full age beneficially entitled with an interest in possession to the trust land. The delegation must be by power of attorney given by all the trustees and may be revoked by any one of them. The delegation may be made for any period of time or indefinitely. This cannot, however, be an "enduring power of attorney" (which deals with permanent delegation when a trustee is mentally incapable). Beneficiaries, to whom the powers have been delegated have the same duties and liabilities as the trustees. They are not, however, regarded as trustees for any other purpose. They cannot sub-delegate their functions nor can they receive capital monies so as to overreach the equitable interest of any beneficiary.

Individual delegation

So far, the emphasis has been upon collective delegation where all the trustees are involved in the appointment of an agent. It is possible that a single trustee will fall ill or be out of the country for some time. In these cases, s.25 of the Trustee Act 1925 (as amended by the Trustee Delegation Act 1999) allows delegation by an individual trustee of all or any of his trust duties, powers and discretions. Restrictions to this ability are as follows:

   (i) delegation must be by power of attorney (*i.e.* it must be made formally in deed form);
  (ii) the period of delegation cannot be for more than 12 months at one time, but special provision is made for an enduring power of attorney when the trustee is mentally incapable of carrying out his functions;
 (iii) the delegating trustee must give written notice to his fellow trustees;
  (iv) the delegating trustee remains liable for the acts and defaults of his attorney as if they were his own acts and defaults.

Section 1 of the Trustee Delegation Act 1999 creates a new statutory power that allows delegation by a trustee to an attorney. The provision extends only to land and can be employed only if the donor also has a beneficial interest in the property. This will be used where there is co-ownership of land and when the trustees are also the beneficiaries. It applies only in the absence of contrary intention in the trust instrument and cannot be invoked when a power of attorney as been given under s.25 of the Trustee Act. The advantages of s.1 are:

  (i) it enables a co-owner trustee to delegate without having to comply with the restrictions that apply where a third party trustee holds land (*e.g.* duty to review);

 (ii) it enables a co-owner to make effective provision for the disposal of the land where the co-owner becomes mentally incapable. An enduring power of attorney is available under this provision;

(iii) it ensures that the donee is able to deal with the proceeds of sale of the land.

---

17.   VARIATION OF TRUSTS

Until the trust is brought to an end, the trustees must carry out the trust according to the terms of the trust instrument and the rules of equity. As a trust may last for years, however, it is possible that the original terms of the trust may become outmoded and unreasonable. In limited circumstances, the law allows the terms of a trust to be varied.

The rule in *Saunders v Vautier*

Provided that they are adult, of sound mind and between themselves are entitled absolutely to the trust property, the beneficiaries may unanimously dismantle the trust or vary its terms. This is known as the rule in *Saunders v Vautier* (1841). The rule cannot apply, therefore, where the beneficiaries are children, include persons not yet born, are not all of sound mind or cannot all be found. In such circumstances, therefore, any intervention will have to be justified instead under either the inherent jurisdiction of the court or the auspices of a statutory provision.

Inherent jurisdiction

Generally the court has no power to authorise a departure from the terms of the trust. As Farwell J. admitted in *Re Walker* (1901),

> "I decline to accept any suggestion that the court has an inherent jurisdiction to alter a man's will because he thinks it beneficial. It seems to me that is quite impossible".

Nevertheless there are situations where an inherent jurisdiction does exist.

1. *Salvage and emergency.* The court has an inherent power to authorise a departure from the terms of a trust where an unforeseen emergency arises or for the purposes of salvage. An example of salvage would be carrying out repairs to prevent a building from collapsing: *Re Jackson* (1882). The variation, however, is limited to giving the trustees increased management and administration powers. It does not extend to variations of beneficial interests: *Chapman v Chapman* (1954).

2. *Compromise.* The court has a limited jurisdiction to approve "compromises" on behalf of minors and unascertained beneficiaries. "Compromises" are given a restricted meaning that requires there to be an element of dispute before the court can interfere. It does not, however, include a mere family arrangement in which a beneficiary gives up a present right in return for a different right: *Chapman v Chapman* (1954). In *Mason v Farbrother* (1983), the trustees of a pension fund applied to the court to give them wider powers of investment than they already possessed. There was a dispute concerning the original investment clause, but the court refused to substitute a new investment clause under its inherent jurisdiction. The courts became wary about the possibility of beneficiaries inventing disputes so that the terms of the trust could be varied.

Statutory jurisdiction

The courts are given wider powers to vary the terms of trusts by a variety of statutory provisions.

1. *Section 57(1) of the Trustee Act 1925.* This provision permits variation of a trust for the purposes of administration and management. The court can intervene where it is expedient to do so even where there is no emergency. Section 57 gives no power to vary the beneficial interests under a trust: *Re Downshire Settled Estates* (1953). The provisions of the section are deemed to be incorporated into every settlement. The section has been used to authorise the sale of chattels, the sale of land where the necessary consents were refused, the purchase of a residence for the tenant for life and to give wider investment powers.

2. Section 64(1) of the Settled Land Act 1925. This section deals with the variation of strict settlements. It gives the court power to sanction departures from the trust that are for the benefit of the land or the beneficiaries provided that they could have been effected by an absolute owner. The section is not limited to management and administration and can be used to alter beneficial interests. Before the enactment of the Variation of Trusts Act 1958, it was often used to minimise tax liability. As, since 1996, no new settlements can be created, this power will eventually be confined to the dustbin of legal history.

3. The Variation of Trusts Act 1958. This Act was passed because of the decision in *Chapman v Chapman* (1954) where the House of Lords refused to vary the beneficial interests of a trust under the court's inherent jurisdiction to compromise claims (see above). The 1958 Act confers a jurisdiction on the High Court to approve an arrangement varying or revoking all or part of an expressly created private trust. The trust instrument, moreover, cannot exclude this jurisdiction.

Under the Act variations can be made covering not only administrative matters, but also beneficial interests, provided always that the arrangement is for the benefit of the person on whose behalf the court is giving approval. Indeed, the Act has been used for a variety of purposes, including inserting a power of advancement, terminating an accumulation and inserting an accumulation period. It is, however, most often used to achieve tax saving variations.

The persons on whose behalf the court may approve a variation are set out in s.1(1) of 1958 Act. As the Act is based upon consent, it is thought that only adult beneficiaries can apply for a variation order. Trustees should make an application only if they believe that the variation will benefit the beneficiaries and there is no adult beneficiary prepared to make an application. The beneficiaries should be unanimous. If not, the non-consenting beneficiaries should be joined as defendants.

The 1958 Act lists four types of beneficiary on whose behalf the court can itself give consent. These are persons under a disability (*e.g.* a minor or person of unsound mind); the unborn; discretionary beneficiaries under protective trusts; and persons with mere expectations. For example, in *Re Suffert* (1951) income was given on protective trusts to a woman for life and on her death, subject to a general testamentary power, to those entitled under the rules of intestacy. She had three adult cousins who were entitled. One cousin was made a party and consented. The court refused to consent on behalf of the other two who were not before the court. Another reason for the failure of the application was that the cousins had an interest, albeit remote and contingent, so that they could not be described as persons "who may become entitled . . . to an interest under a trust".

"Benefit" does not just mean financial benefit, although variations are usually made to save tax. In *Re Weston's Settlements* (1969), Lord Denning said,

> "The court should not consider merely the financial benefit to the infant and unborn children but also their educational and social benefit. There are many things in life more worthwhile than money".

In *Re Remnant's Settlement Trusts* (1970), the removal of a forfeiture provision, activated on becoming a practising Roman Catholic, was a benefit for its retention could cause trouble within the family. It has also been held that it would benefit a mentally handicapped person to give away his property if that is what he would have done had he been of sound mind: *Re C.L.* (1969). The benefit, moreover, does not have to be a certainty, for what is required is a reasonable chance that it will occur. Thus arrangements have been made which depend on a woman having no more children or a life-tenant dying before a particular date: *Re Cohen's Settlement* (1976). In deciding upon benefit, the court does not have to take into account the testator's intentions: *Goulding v James* (1997).

The Act does no more than give the court power to consent to arrangements on behalf of those unable to consent themselves. Adult ascertained beneficiaries have to give their own consent. The legal result is that the variation of the trust is effected not by the court, but by the consent of the parties: *Re Holt's Settlement* (1969). The variation takes effect as soon as the order is made by the court and no further instrument is needed. The old trusts are simply replaced by new trusts.

4. ***Matrimonial Causes Act 1973.*** The court has wide powers to make orders concerning the allocation of property between the parties in matrimonial proceedings. These powers include varying ante-nuptial and post-nuptial settlements for the benefit of the parties to the marriage and their children. In *Brooks v Brooks* (1999), the husband's pension scheme was varied for the benefit of a divorced wife.

5. ***Mental Health Act 1983.*** This Act gives the Court of Protection the power to make a settlement of a patient's property and to vary such settlements should there be any substantial change in circumstances (*e.g.* if the person ceases to be of unsound mind).

18. BREACH OF TRUST

A trustee is liable for both acts of omission (failing to do what he ought to do) and acts of commission (doing what he should not do). Breaches of trust by a trustee fall within three broad categories: gaining an unauthorised profit; failing to act with care and skill in the administration of the trust; and misapplications of trust property. The trustee has a liability either to compensate for loss or to account for gains subsequent to the breach. The essential principle is the same whether the trust is express or implied. Not surprisingly, the beneficiaries have a number of remedies against the trustee for a breach of trust. In addition, the beneficiary might be able to exercise remedies against third parties. The aim of these remedies is to ensure that the breach is redressed as far as is possible.

Liability of a trustee for his own acts

If the trustee commits a breach of trust, he is liable to the trust for any loss incurred or personal gain made. A trustee is not, however, liable for breaches of trust committed by his predecessors. He should, however, sort out any irregularities he discovers when taking office, including obtaining satisfaction from the old trustees. If the trustee fails to do so, he may himself be liable for loss arising from this omission. If the trustee takes the appropriate steps on appointment, he is entitled to assume that there has been no pre-existing breach of trust.

On retirement, a trustee (or, if he is deceased, his estate) will still remain liable for breaches of trust that occurred during his stewardship. Generally, a trustee is not liable for breaches committed by his successors unless his retirement occurred so that the breach could be committed or to avoid his becoming involved with it. Mere recognition that his retirement would facilitate a breach is not sufficient: *Head v Gould* (1898).

Liability for acts of co-trustees

A trustee can never be vicariously liable for the acts of another trustee. Liability can, however, arise when the trustee himself is at fault in allowing another trustee to commit a breach. The yardstick is whether the "innocent" trustee acted as a prudent man of business and is not limited to acts of willful default.

A trustee will be liable for a breach of trust resulting from the act or omission of a co-trustee in the following situations:

(i)   leaving trust income in the hands of a co-trustee for too long without making proper inquiries: *Townley v Sherborne* (1634);

(ii) concealing a breach committed by his fellow trustees: *Boardman v Mossman* (1779); and

(iii) standing by while to his knowledge a breach of trust is being committed (*Booth v Booth* (1838)) or contemplated (*Wilkins v Hogg* (1861)).

Equitable compensation

The main remedy of the beneficiary is to claim equitable compensation for breach of trust. The claimant, however, may only recover for loss caused by the defendant's breach: *Target Holdings Ltd v Redfearns* (1996). This remedy is available whether or not there has been some misappropriation of trust property by the trustee: *Nocton v Lord Ashburton* (1914). This is demonstrated in the following examples relating to the trust capital:

(i)   where a trustee makes an unauthorised investment, he is liable for the loss incurred when it is sold: *Knott v Cottee* (1852);

(ii) where the trustee wrongfully retains an unauthorised investment, he is liable for the difference between the price he obtains when it is sold and the price that would have been obtained had he sold it at the right time: *Fry v Fry* (1859);

(iii) where a trustee improperly realises an authorised investment, he must replace it or pay the difference between the price obtained and the cost of repurchasing the investment: *Phillipson v Gatty* (1848). Where the court has to assess the cost of replacing the investment, it will be valued at the date of judgment: *Re Bell's Indenture* (1980);

(iv) if a profit arises from a breach of trust the beneficiaries can claim it: *Daker v Somes* (1834). A trustee, moreover, cannot claim that a profit made in one transaction should be set off against a loss suffered in another transaction: *Dimes v Scott* (1828). If, however, the gain and loss are part of the same transaction, then the rule against set-off will not apply: *Fletcher v Green* (1864). For example, in *Bartlett v Barclays Bank Trust Co Ltd* (1980) the bank was able to set off the losses on a development project at the Old Bailey against the profits made on another development at Guildford. Both resulted from a policy of unauthorised speculative investments.

As well as repaying the capital the trustee is liable to pay interest to the trust fund where the loss results from an unauthorised investment or payment of the trust estate to the wrong person. He must also pay interest where he is guilty of undue delay in investing the trust funds. The rate of interest remains at the discretion of the court. Nevertheless, it is likely to be either 1 per cent above the base rate of lending (*Wallersteiner v Moir (No.2)* (1975)) or the prevailing rate of the court's short term investment account (*Bartlett v Barclays Bank Trust Co Ltd* (1980)). Simple interest will generally be awarded, but in exceptional circumstances it can be compounded annually (*e.g.* when under a duty to accumulate the trust income).

Any beneficial interest a trustee has can be withheld to make good his breach of trust: *Re Dacre* (1916).

Joint and several liability

Where two or more trustees are each liable for a breach of trust, they are jointly and severally liable. This means that any one of the trustees may be sued for the full amount or, if they all are sued, judgment may be executed against any one (or more) of them. At common law, all trustees who were in breach were liable equally and, if one had paid more than his share, he could claim a contribution from the others. Under the Civil (Liability) Contribution Act 1978, however, the court has a wide discretion to fix the amount of contribution from a co-trustee depending upon what is fair and reasonable in all the circumstances.

The 1978 Act also broadened the circumstances in which a trustee can be completely indemnified by one or more of his co-trustees. Indemnity is appropriate where:

(i) one trustee acted fraudulently or was alone morally culpable: *Bahin v Hughes* (1886);

(ii) the breach was committed solely on the advice of a solicitor co-trustee: *Head v Gould* (1898);

(iii) only one trustee has benefited from the breach: *Bahin v Hughes* (1886) and,

(iv) one of the trustees was also a beneficiary: *Chillingworth v Chambers* (1896).

Under the Limitation Act 1980, the trustees have two years within which to claim a contribution. Time runs either from the date of judgment against a trustee or from the date when the trustee settles the beneficiary's claim.

If a trustee overpays a beneficiary the trustee can adjust the accounts by making deductions from future income: *Liversey v Liversey* (1827). If he underpays himself and overpays others, however, he cannot adjust the accounts if this would cause hardship to the beneficiaries.

Protection of trustees from liability

The trust instrument may restrict or extend the liability of a trustee. In *Armitage v Nurse* (1997), an express exemption protecting a trustee "from any cause whatsoever unless such loss or damage shall be caused by his own actual fraud" was upheld. It would not, therefore, cover dishonesty on the part of a trustee. It does, however, extend to cover negligence. The Law Commission believes that such clauses should be invalid in the case of paid, professional trustees.

Under s.57 of the Trustee Act 1925, a trustee may apply to the court for authorisation to effect a dealing with the trust property not permitted by the trust instrument (see Ch.17). If the court sanctions the proposed act, then there is no breach of trust. If the act has already been carried out before an application to court is made, the court enjoys a discretion given by s.61.

Under s.61, the court may relieve a trustee from liability if he

"acted honestly and reasonably, and ought fairly to be excused for the breach of trust and for omitting to obtain the directions of the court in the matter in which he committed such breach".

There are no rules when relief will be granted and each case will be judged on its own particular circumstances: *Re Evans* (1999). The burden lies on the trustee to establish that he acted reasonably and honestly and as prudently as he would have done in organising his own affairs. As Harman J. explained in *Re Waterman's Will Trusts* (1952), "a paid trustee is expected to exercise a higher standard of diligence and knowledge than an unpaid trustee". This distinction now has statutory recognition in s.1 of the Trustee Act 2000.

(i) In *Re Kay* (1897), the testator left £22,000. The apparent liabilities of the estate were £100. The trustee advertised for creditors of the estate, having previously given the widow £300. It turned out that the testator's debts amounted to more than £22,000. The court held that the trustee had acted honestly and reasonably. It was unforeseeable that the actual debts would be more than £22,000 when the apparent debts were £100.

(ii) Obtaining legal advice before acting may not alone be sufficient to bring the trustee within s.61. In *National Trustees Co of Australasia Ltd v General Finance Co* (1905), the trustees followed the advice of a solicitor which was incorrect. The trust was large and complicated and the court held that the advice of a trust expert, a senior counsel, should have been sought.

A trustee may be immune from liability following bankruptcy. The Insolvency Act 1986 provides that, where a bankrupt trustee has obtained his discharge from bankruptcy, he will be freed from further liability. This does not apply, however, where the trustee was a party to a fraudulent breach of trust.

The normal rule is that an action for breach of trust must be brought within six years of either the breach of trust, the beneficiary's interest vesting in possession or the beneficiary obtaining his majority, whichever is the later.

(i) The Limitation Act 1980, however, states that no limitation period applies to an action by a beneficiary in two
situations. First, "in respect of any fraud or fraudulent
breach of trust to which the trustee was a party or privy".
Secondly, "to recover from the trustee the trust property
or the proceeds thereof in the possession of the trustee or
previously received by the trustee and converted to his
use". The doctrine of laches may apply: *Nelson v Rye*
(1996).

(ii) A trustee, who is also a beneficiary, is, after the limitation
period, only liable to replace the excess over his proper
share. This relief is available only where he acted reasonably in making the distribution, *Re Somerset* (1894).

(iii) The limitation period does not apply to a claim by the
Attorney-General against the trustee of a charitable trust
which has no "beneficiary": *Att-Gen v Cocke* (1988).

Acts of beneficiaries

A beneficiary who has consented to or participates in a breach
of trust cannot afterwards sue the trustees for breach of trust.
This rule applies when three conditions are satisfied:

(i) the beneficiary was of full age and sound mind at the time
of agreement or concurrence;

(ii) the beneficiary had full knowledge of the relevant facts
and of the legal effect of his actions;

(iii) the beneficiary acted voluntarily and was not under the
undue influence of another.

In *Nail v Punter* (1832), the trustees held stock on trust for a
woman for life, with remainder to such person as she should by
will appoint. Her husband persuaded her to sell the stock in
breach of trust. She died and appointed her husband as her
beneficiary. It was held that he could not sue the trustees
because he had been a party to the breach of trust.

In *Re Pauling's Settlement Trusts* (1964), a bank was a trustee
for a woman for life, with remainder to her children. The bank
advanced money to the (now adult) children, but their parents
misapplied the funds. The children later sought to recover the
money from the trustee bank. As a result of undue influence
exerted by their father, the children had not been fully aware of
the nature of their entitlements and, therefore, could succeed.

The court has an inherent jurisdiction to order that a trustee or other beneficiaries be indemnified out of the interest of a beneficiary who instigated or requested such a breach. If the beneficiary merely concurred in the breach, it must be shown he received a benefit from it: *Montford v Cadogan* (1816). This is supplemented by s.62 of the Trustee Act 1925 which states:

> "Where a trustee commits a breach of trust at the instigation or request or with the consent in writing of a beneficiary, the court may, if it thinks fit . . . make such order as to the court seems just, for impounding all or any part of the interest of the beneficiary in the trust estate by way of indemnity to the trustee or persons claiming through him."

This provision operates regardless of personal benefit.

Tracing and third parties

Tracing involves getting the actual property back, or the asset that represents it. If property gets into the hands of B, A can, in certain circumstances, trace the property and reclaim it from B. Tracing is a proprietary remedy. As Lord Millett said in *Foskett v McKeown* (2001), ". . . this branch of the law is concerned with vindicating rights of property." The defences to a tracing claim are that the claimant's property is not in the stranger's hands or that the stranger was a bona fide purchaser for value of the property. It is, however, no defence to show that the recipient has substituted the claimant's property (in whole or in part) for other property.

Tracing has several advantages over a mere personal claim:

(i) it may be available where there is no effective personal claim as where the trustee is insolvent and the person who has the property is an innocent volunteer;

(ii) if the person, B, who has the property goes bankrupt then the owner, A, can claim priority over B's creditors. A is a secured creditor as he has a proprietary claim which is attached to the property;

(iii) claimants are entitled to any income produced by the assets that have been traced from the date on which the property came into the defendant's hands. This is in contrast with claims *in personam* that only carry interest from the date of judgment). In some cases the claimant will not just be entitled to the return of his money but also to any increase in the value of the property.

Tracing (following) at common law

At common law, following the property was possible as long as it was not mixed with other property. Hence, once money is mixed, as in a bank account, there can be no tracing at common law. Thus only identifiable tangible property could be followed, as could a chose in action (*e.g.* a bank balance) or property purchased with the claimant's money. In *Taylor v Plummer* (1815), for example, the defendant handed money to his stockbroker to purchase exchequer bonds. The stockbroker purchased American investments instead. On the stockbroker's bankruptcy, the defendant was entitled to the investments that represented the money he had given to the stockbroker. Another limitation of common law was that it did not recognise equitable rights. A beneficiary under a trust could not at law follow his property into the hands of the trustees.

Tracing in equity

Tracing in equity is possible when there is an equity to trace, the property is traceable and the tracing does not produce an inequitable result.

1. *An equity to trace.* In order for the remedy to be available, there must be some initial fiduciary relationship. It is not sufficient merely to show that the defendant has been unjustly enriched. In *Lister v Stubbs* (1890), the defendant was the plaintiff's agent. He received secret commissions (bribes). Part of this money he invested in land. The plaintiff was unable to follow the money because there was not a fiduciary relationship, only a contractual one between the principal and agent. There was no equity to trace. A similar principle applied in *Re Att-Gen's Reference (No.1)* (1985) where a publican made a secret profit by selling his own beer in breach of his contract with the brewer. However *Lister v Stubbs* was disapproved of by the House of Lords in *Att-Gen for Hong Kong v Reid* (1993). There a solicitor acting for the Hong Kong Government received bribes. He was held liable to account for the bribes and for the increased value of the property representing the bribes. Lord Templeman determined that the *Lister* Case,

> ". . . is not consistent with the principles that a fiduciary must not be allowed to benefit from his own breach of duty . . . the bribe and the property from time to time representing the bribe are held on constructive trust for the person injured."

This approach is based upon notions of public policy.

The most obvious example of a fiduciary relationship is between a trustee and a beneficiary but sometimes the contract itself will give rise to a fiduciary relationship. In *Aluminium Industrie Vaasen BV v Romalpa Aluminium Ltd* (1976), the plaintiff company sold aluminium foil to Romalpa. A term of the contract was that ownership in the aluminium would pass to Romalpa only when Romalpa completed payment. On the liquidation of Romalpa, and before payment to the plaintiff had been completed, the plaintiff company was held entitled to trace money in Romalpa's account which represented the proceeds of sale of the foil to sub-purchasers. Since *Romalpa* the courts have been reluctant to uphold fiduciary relationships of this kind: *Tatung (UK) Ltd v Galex Telesure Ltd* (1989). A retention clause will only operate so as to give the seller of goods an interest in any proceeds of sub-sale if registered as a security charge under the Companies Act 1985.

An extreme example of the court finding a fiduciary relationship is *Chase Manhattan Bank NA v Israel British Bank (London) Ltd* (1981). The Chase Manhattan Bank paid money to another bank by mistake. That bank paid the money to the Israel British Bank, which then went into liquidation. It was held that the Chase Manhattan Bank had a continuing equitable proprietary right in the money that enabled it to trace and acquire priority over the general creditors. The mistaken payment to the defendant itself gave rise to the fiduciary relationship. In *Westdeutsche Landesbank Girozentrale v Islington BC* (1996), however, the House of Lords held that the bank did not have an equitable proprietary interest in money paid under an *ultra vires* void transaction.

In *Agip (Africa) Ltd v Jackson* (1989) Millett J. said:

> "The requirement [that there must be some fiduciary relationship] is . . . readily satisfied in most cases of commercial fraud, since the embezzlement of a company's funds almost inevitably involves a breach of fiduciary duty on the part of one of the company's employees or agents."

2. The property must be traceable. It may be easy to trace money as where it has been invested in shares. In this case, the beneficiary can claim either the property itself or a charge on it for the money expended in the purchase: *Sinclair v Brougham* (1914). It is sometimes impossible to trace as where the money has been dissipated on living expenses. In *Re Diplock* (1948), it was held impossible to trace property used to pay off loans. This was distinguished in *Boscawen v Bajwa* (1995) where a building society was entitled to trace money advanced to pay off an existing loan and was subrogated to the position of the original mortgagee.

The difficulty arises where money has been mixed and the separate funds cannot be identified. There are various rules for dealing with the problem.

(i) The onus is on the trustee to establish what is trust property and what is his own. If he cannot do this then the whole will be treated as trust property: *Lupton v White* (1808).

(ii) If a trustee mixes the funds of two trusts (or an innocent volunteer mixes his own funds and that of a trust in a single bank account), the rule in *Clayton's Case* (1816) may be applied. The first payment out is set against the first payment in and vice versa; "first in first out" unless there is an express appropriation. The rule can be excluded expressly by agreement or by implication from the circumstances.

(iii) Where a trustee mixes trust funds with his own the rule in *Re Hallett's Estate* (1880) may be applied. A trustee is presumed to draw on his own money first before using the trust money. He is not expected to want to commit a breach of trust. It is only when his own money is exhausted that he is taken to be drawing trust funds. For example: a trustee has £1,000 in an account, £500 of his own funds, £500 of trust funds. He then spends £500 on a holiday. The £500 spent is deemed to be his own money. *Re Hallett*, therefore, operates to displace the rule in *Clayton's Case.*

(iv) Where a trustee draws out more than his own money and is, therefore, spending some of the trust funds any money subsequently paid in will not, without express appropriation, go to restoring the trust funds. To continue with the example given in (iii) above, if the trustee dissipates a further £400 and later pays in £200 of his own money, the beneficiaries cannot claim this amount. They can claim only the lowest intermediate balance, namely £100: *James Roscoe (Bolton) Ltd v Winder* (1915).

(v) *Re Hallett* is subject to the overriding principle that the beneficiary has a first charge on any property bought out of a mixed fund. In *Re Oatway* (1903), a trustee withdrew money from a mixed fund and invested it. Later he withdrew the rest of the money, which he then dissipated. In such circumstances, the creditors could not successfully claim that the trustee was deemed to spend his own money first. The beneficiaries were, instead, entitled to the investments and any profit made on them.

(vi) Any trust money paid into the trustee's bank account to reduce the trustee's overdraft must be repaid. The debt will be charged on any properties purchased with the help of the overdraft, but the beneficiaries will not be able to claim any part of the properties themselves. The reason being that the money is used to repay the debt, not to purchase the property: *Re Tilley's Will Trusts* (1967).

(vii) Different considerations apply in cases other than bank accounts. If a trustee mixes funds of different trusts (or a volunteer mixes his own money with trust funds) and identification is not possible, the beneficiaries under the respective trusts (or the beneficiary and the volunteer) will have a charge on any property bought with the mixed funds. They will share the charge rateably *(pari passu)*.

(viii) If an innocent volunteer mixes his own money with trust money and the property increases in value then the increase will be shared rateably. Accordingly, a beneficiary should be entitled to a proportion of the increase where a trustee mixes funds of his own with trust funds: *Re Tilley's Wills Trusts* (1967). If it were otherwise the trustee would be profiting from his breach of trust.

3. *Tracing must not produce an inequitable result.* The consequences of this rule are that:

(i) a right to trace cannot be exercised against a bona fide purchaser for value without notice of the equity;

(ii) no claimant can trace who has acquiesced in the wrongful mixing or distribution;

(iii) no tracing will be allowed where it would cause injustice. For example, if an innocent volunteer improves his own house with the use of trust money then tracing will not be allowed. It would result in the sale of the house. If he had bought a house, however, partly with trust money, tracing will be allowed for both he and the beneficiaries can be restored to their original positions by the repayment of money: *Foskett v McKeown* (2001). The latter is analogous to the mixture of monies in a bank account.

Most of the principles of tracing are illustrated in *Re Diplock* (1948). By his will, Caleb Diplock gave his residuary estate to "such charitable institutions or other charitable or benevolent objects as my executors may in their absolute discretion select." The executors, thinking this was a valid charitable gift, distributed £203,000 amongst various charities. The next of kin succeeded in their claim to trace against the charities by establishing a fiduciary relationship between themselves and the executors. There was held to be nothing inequitable in tracing property into the hands of innocent charitable institutions. It was, however, considered to be impracticable to trace funds that had been spent on improving part of a building in the middle of a hospital. Where the charities held the funds without mixing with other funds, all the money was held for the next of kin. Where the money had been mixed the charity and the next of kin shared *pari passu*.

Personal remedy: *Re Diplock*

When an executor, in winding up the deceased's estate, wrongfully distributes the estate, a personal action may be brought against the recipient for the overpayment: *Re Diplock* (1948). This personal action is available to an unpaid legatee, creditor or next of kin. It is not available to beneficiaries under an *inter vivos* (lifetime) trust. This personal claim is enforceable only to the extent that the money is not recoverable from the negligent executor.

Knowing receipt and dishonest assistance

If a third party has received trust property, but has not retained it, the remedy of tracing is inappropriate. A beneficiary, however, might be able to bring a personal action against the recipient if he had received the trust property knowing (or subsequently discovering) that it was trust property (*i.e.* knowing receipt). If a third party did not receive trust property at all, accessory liability might arise for dishonest assistance in the breach of trust.

1. *Knowing receipt.* This concerns what Lord Nicholls referred to in *Royal Brunei Airlines v Tan* (1995) as, ". . . the liability of a person as a recipient of trust property or its traceable proceeds." Liability will arise only if there is the right type of "knowledge" and the right type of "receipt".

A person who receives property innocently, but later discovers that it is trust property, becomes liable to account from that discovery. If the recipient parts with the property before ever knowing that it was trust property, there is no liability. As Millett L.J. admitted in *Agip (Africa) Ltd v Jackson* (1990), ". . . the true distinction is between honesty and dishonesty."

Although these categories are not precise and always clear cut, there are several types of knowledge as set out by Peter Gibson L.J. in the *Baden Case* (1993):

(i) actual knowledge;
(ii) willfully shutting one's eyes to the obvious;
(iii) willfully and recklessly failing to make reasonable inquiries;
(iv) knowledge of circumstances which would indicate the facts to a reasonable man;
(v) knowledge of facts which would put a reasonable man on inquiry.

There has to be some dishonesty, want of probity or unconscionability before personal liability can ensue. There has to be more than a genuine misunderstanding or mistake: *Re Montagu's Settlement Trusts* (1987). It is necessary to show that the defendant's conduct was inconsistent with how an honest man would have behaved in the circumstances: *Hillsdown Holdings plc v Pensions Ombudsman* (1997). There is no need, however, to show that the recipient was actually dishonest: *Bank of Credit and Commerce International Ltd v Akindele* (2001).

2. Dishonest assistance. This is a form of accessory or secondary liability that arises from merely assisting a trustee to breach the terms of the trust. Since *Royal Brunei Airlines v Tan* (1995), the court has looked at the nature of the assistance provided. It is not necessary that the trustee acted dishonestly or fraudulently.

The meaning of dishonesty came before the House of Lords in *Twinsectra Ltd v Yardley* (2002). It was held that the test for dishonesty was a hybrid (or combined test) of subjective and objective elements. This entails that a defendant will be personally liable as an accessory if it can be shown that he knew that what he was doing was dishonest by the standards of an honest and reasonable man. There has to be more than unconscionability as regards accessory liability.

---

19. EXAMINATION CHECKLIST

1. What are the main statutes which govern trusts?
2. What are the principles set out in the case of *Keech v Sandford* (1726), *Saunders v Vautier* (1841), *McPhail v Doulton* (1971), *Commissioners of Income Tax v Pemsel* (1891), *Learoyd v Whiteley* (1886) and *Re Diplock* (1948)? Think of six other significant cases.
3. Are the three certainties satisfied to created a trust?
4. Is the trust properly constituted?
5. Have the proper formalities been observed?
6. What are the distinctions between a fully and half secret trust?
7. When can trusts be set aside?
8. When will a protective trust be used?
9. What are the two types of resulting trust?
10. What is the distinction between a resulting trust and a constructive trust?
11. What are the categories of non-charitable purpose trusts that have bee upheld?
12. What are the different ways a gift to an unincorporated association may be construed?
13. What are the four heads of charitable trusts?
14. What are the problems about public benefit and political purposes?
15. What is the doctrine of cy-pres?
16. What is the maximum number of trustees?
17. Who appoints them and what are the different rules for replacement and additional trustees?
18. What new provisions on appointment and retirement of trustees were introduced by the Trusts of Land and Appointment of New Trustees Act 1996?
19. What are the guiding principles when considering the duties of trustees?
20. What are the rules on maintenance, advancement and delegation?

21. When can a trust be varied?
22. How may a trustee escape liability for breach of trust?
23. When is tracing possible?
24. What are the conflicting views on the need for a fiduciary relationship?
25. In what circumstances may a third party be liable for knowing receipt and dishonest assistance?

20. SAMPLE QUESTIONS AND MODEL ANSWERS

Question 1

Gladstone and Bower are trustees of a trust of land which they hold for the benefit of Zoe and Foster as tenants in common. Part of the land consists of a farmhouse that Zoe wants to occupy. Gladstone has no objection to this, but Bower does. Zoe would like to have Bower removed as a trustee. She would also like to control the trust property and not have to rely on the trustees.

Advise Zoe.

Answer

The issues raised in this question relate to a beneficiary's right of occupation, the power of a beneficiary to remove a trustee and the delegation of a trustee's powers.

1. The right of occupation. Section 12(1) of the Trusts of Land and Appointment of Trustees Act 1996 provides:

"A beneficiary who is beneficially entitled to an interest in possession in land subject to a trust of land is entitled by reason of his interest to occupy the land at any time if at that time:

(a) The purposes of the trust include making the land available for his occupation (or for the occupation of beneficiaries of the class of which he is a member or of beneficiaries in general) or
(b) The land is held by the trustees so as to be so available."

Zoe would appear to be entitled to an interest in possession, having a present right of present enjoyment, and so *prima facie* is entitled to occupy the land. However, the rights conferred by s.12(1) do not apply if the land is either unavailable or unsuitable. If the farmhouse is part of a working farm and Zoe has no farming experience, she will have no automatic right of occupation.

Foster is also entitled to an interest in possession. The trustees could decide that he should be given the right to occupy the property. Under s.13 the trustees can restrict or exclude the right of occupation where two or more beneficiaries are entitled. They can also impose reasonable conditions, including the payment of outgoings and compensation. In exercising the power to exclude or restrict occupation, the trustees have to consider, amongst other things, the intentions of the person who created the trust, the purposes for which the land is held and the circumstances and wishes of each of the beneficiaries who is entitled to occupy the land.

2. Directions for the removal of a trustee.   Where there is no person nominated for the purpose of appointing new trustees by the trust instrument, and the beneficiaries under the trust are of full age and capacity and together are absolutely entitled to the property subject to the trust, beneficiaries may give a direction for the retirement or appointment of a trustee. In this case, as there are only two trustees, if directions are going to be given for the retirement of Bower, then another trustee would have to be appointed.

However, in order to give an effective direction, the beneficiaries must be unanimous. If Foster is happy with Bower as a trustee and does not want to join in with the direction, then Zoe will not be able to insist on the retirement of Bower.

3. Delegation.   Under s.9 of the Trusts of Land and Appointment of Trustees Act 1996, trustees are given wide powers to delegate to any beneficiary or beneficiaries of full age beneficially entitled to an interest in possession in the trust property any of their functions as trustees which relate to the land. A delegation is by Power of Attorney. The delegation could be given to Zoe alone, rather than to both the beneficiaries. However, the delegation must be made by all the trustees. It appears unlikely from the facts that Bower would agree to such a delegation.

Although once the delegation has taken place the trustees are not liable for any default of the beneficiary, they can be liable if they do not exercise reasonable care in deciding to delegate the function in the first place. As part of the general law, trustees are under a duty to hold the balance between the beneficiaries. It appears from the facts that Zoe is making the demands and the trustees before delegating should make sure that the interests of Foster are properly protected.

Even if the power of sale were delegated to Zoe any capital money would have to be paid to the trustees and not to her personally.

Question 2

Advise the organisation known as Feminists For Freedom (FFF) on whether its charter's aims entitled it to charitable status.

(1) The FFF seeks to promote a greater understanding of feminist literature, to which end it seeks to publish works by female authors, including books dealing with prostitution. The FFF also seeks to establish a feminist library for FFF staff and their families.

(2) The FFF seeks to provide accommodation for female single parents on 60–year non-assignable leases at below market price for those who would otherwise be homeless and therefore in need. The FFF does not seek to make a profit from the provision of accommodation and any surplus funds will be used to provide child care facilities for the single mothers.

(3) The FFF seeks, through lobbying and peaceful demonstration, to change the law relating to gender discrimination and equal pay in this country and abroad and thereby alleviate the lot of all women and improve their life in general.

(4) The FFF seeks to assist the campaign to allow the ordination of women in the Roman Catholic Church in the belief that this will increase the size of congregations.

(5) The FFF seeks to advance the study by girls and women at schools and institutions of further and higher education in engineering, law, computer sciences, physics and other studies usually associated with men.

What difficulties, if any, will there be in the event that only some of the clauses are deemed charitable?

Answer

In order for the FFF to achieve charitable status it must show that its objects are exclusively charitable and have a sufficient element of public benefit. There is not a legal definition of what is a charitable purpose but the courts pay attention to the charitable objects specified in the Charitable Uses Act 1601 even though this Act has now been repealed. These purposes have been summarised by Lord Macnaghten in *Commissioners of Income Tax v Pemsel* (1891) as trusts for (1) relief of poverty; (2) advancement of religion; (3) advancement of education; and (4) other purposes beneficial to the community that do not fall under any of the other heads.

Clause (1)

This clause could constitute a trust for the advancement of education. Education is not confined to the classroom *(Re Hopkins* (1965)). Pornography as such would not be educational in this sense *(Re Pinion* (1965)). It is unlikely that books published by feminists would be pornographic. They are more likely to have a serious social purpose. The library although educational would not be charitable as it is restricted to FFF staff and their families. It would therefore not be of general public benefit *(Oppenheim v Tobacco Securities Trust Co Ltd* (1951)). As the library is not an ancillary purpose, the whole clause would fail. There is no legislation in this country as there is in Australia and New Zealand to strike out the non-charitable elements.

Clause (2)

There can be no effective charitable trust under the heading of poverty if the gift could benefit the rich as well as the poor *(Re Gwyon* (1931)). Single female parents are not necessarily poor, but the facts of the question do state that "they would otherwise be homeless and therefore in need". In *Joseph Rowntree Memorial Trust Housing Association Ltd v Att-Gen* (1983), it was held that the fact that the accommodation was provided by way of bargain on a contractual basis rather than by way of bounty did not prevent the trust from being charitable. Nor did it matter that the length of the leases might outlast the needs of the beneficiaries as they might well do on the facts of the question. The position would be different if FFF intended to profit from the arrangement and not to use such profit for charitable purposes.

Clause (3)

Prima facie this would come under the fourth charitable head, namely a trust for purposes beneficial to the community. However changing the law is a political purpose and political purposes are not charitable *(McGovern v Att-Gen* (1982)). This rule applies where the aim is to change the law or government policy at home or abroad.

Clause (4)

It could be argued that this creates a trust for the advancement of religion. Larger congregations mean more people going out into the world to "mix with their fellow citizens" *(Neville Estates Ltd v Madden* (1962)). On the other hand, there would need to be a change in canon law to allow women priests and this aim might therefore fail, being tainted with a political purpose.

Clause (5)

This would succeed as a trust for education being for the benefit of a sufficiently large section of the community. It does not matter that the trust is for women only. Section 43 of the Sex Discrimination Act 1975 provides that the Act does not apply to any provision in a charitable trust conferring benefits on one sex only.

If any one of the clauses is non-charitable then FFF would not acquire charitable status *(Oxford Group v Inland Revenue Commissioners* (1949)). It would be otherwise if a fully charitable purpose incidentally conferred a benefit on objects that are not charitable *(Re Coxen* (1948)). FFF should redraft cl.2 so that the library is available to the public at large and delete cll.3 and 4. The taxation advantages would make this exercise worthwhile.

Question 3

Buster leaves all his property to his wife "secure in the knowledge that upon her death anything she has that came from me she will leave to such of my relatives and such of those persons she knows to be my old friends as she should think fit."

Discuss whether this establishes a valid trust.

Answer

In order to create a valid trust the three certainties must be established; certainty of intention, subject-matter and objects *(Knight v Knight* (1840)).

It is possible on the wording that Buster did not intend to impose a trust on his widow but merely to express a hope that she might deal with the property in a certain way *(Re Adams & The Kingston Vestry* (1884)). It is not necessary that he should have used the word trust but the words must be strong enough to impose an obligation on her. The fact that Buster did not leave his widow a mere life interest in the property or restrict her dealing with it in any way suggests an absolute gift. On the other hand construing the will as a whole may lead to the conclusion that he intended a trust.

The subject-matter of the trust is clear in that Buster left his entire estate to his wife, not using vague words like "the bulk of my estate" *(Palmer v Simmonds* (1854)). However it is not clear what is the size of the beneficial interests. It may be that the wife should have only a life interest *(Re Last* (1958)). In such a case though entitled to the income she would not be entitled to the capital. In *Sprange v Barnard* (1789) where a testatrix left her property to her husband Sprange for his sole use and "at his death the remaining part of what is left, that he does not want for his own wants and uses," to be left to others, the court held Sprange was absolutely entitled to the property on the ground that "the property and the person to whom it is to be given must be certain in order to raise a trust". Another possibility is that there might be a floating trust as in *Ottaway v Norman* (1972) that would crystallise only on the death of the widow. During her lifetime she could deal with the property as an absolute owner but on her death she would have to leave it according to Buster's directions. On the wording of this particular trust the widow would be under a fiduciary duty not to dispose of the assets of the trust, or a substantial part of them, so as to defeat the interests of the friends and relatives.

The trust for the friends and relatives is a discretionary trust so there is no need for a complete list of beneficiaries *(Mcphail v Doulton* (1971)). It must however be possible to say of any given person that he is or is not a relative or friend. Taking relatives to mean next of kin *(per* Stamp L.J. in *Re Baden* (1973)), the class is conceptually certain but old friends is too vague. In *Re Barlow's Will Trusts* (1979) Browne-Wilkinson J. gave some guidelines on friends. He said:

"(a) the relationship must have been a long-standing one; (b) the relationship must have been a social relationship as opposed to a business or professional relationship; (c) although there may have been long periods when circumstances prevented the testatrix and the applicant from meeting, when circumstances did permit they must have met frequently".

He was however dealing with gifts subject to a condition precedent where it seems the rules as to certainty of objects are less stringent. Moreover in this case there is a further difficulty in that the friends have to be old friends. This would mean that the class would be conceptually uncertain were it not for the provision that the widow is to decide who were the testator's old friends. It is permissible for a third party to determine who should be within the class *(Re Tuck Settlement Trusts* (1976), questions of Jewish blood and faith should be determined by the chief rabbi). Taking the whole clause together it appears that the testator did not wish to restrict his widow's use of the property during her life and was happy to rely on her judgment for its disposal on her death. The tenor of the clause is not to create a trust but to give her an absolute gift on the assumption that she would want on her death to leave the property to his friends and relatives.

Question 4

On November 29, Malcolm told Jane that if she agreed, he hoped that she would, at some future date, act as his trustee, holding on behalf of Nathan. On December 1, Malcolm made his will leaving his home, Dunborin, and £100,000 to Jane "on such trusts as I have indicated to her" and the residue of his estate to Hanbury. On December 2 Malcolm handed Jane a sealed envelope saying that the contents confirmed their conversation of November 29 but that it was only to be opened upon his death.

Three years later in April Jane told Nathan that when Malcolm died he would be a very wealthy person. In July of the same year Nathan became a vegetarian and immediately declared himself trustee of any interests in property he would receive upon Malcolm's death, for the benefit of the National Vegetarian Council, a registered charity.

Nathan died on October 1, choking on a raw carrot. Malcolm did not know of this before his very recent death last month.

Advise Jane, Nathan's estate and the National Vegetarian Council. The letter, when opened, stated that Dunborin and the £100,000 were to be held on trust for Nathan.

Answer

Malcolm's will leaves his home Dunborin and £100,000 to Jane as trustee. There is thus no possibility of Jane taking the property beneficially. Jane will either hold the property on trust for Nathan, if a half secret trust can be established, or if not for Hanbury, who is entitled to Malcolm's residuary estate.

Before a half secret trust will be valid it must be established:

(1) That there has been a sufficient communication of the terms of the trust *before* or *at the same time* as the will. The rule is based on unsatisfactory dicta in *Blackwell v Blackwell* (1929, HL) and has been severely criticised. In fully secret trusts where the trustee appears to take beneficially on the face of the will, communication can take place at any time before the testator's death.

There is no logical reason why this rule should not be the same for half secret trusts.

(2) There must be acceptance of the terms by the trustee.

(3) There must be no conflict between the terms of the will and the secret trust.

It is impossible to tell from the facts whether there was a sufficient communication on November 29. To be effective Jane must have been told of the property to be comprised in the trust (*Re Colin Cooper* (1939)). If not, the subsequent letter will not be a sufficient communication. Although communication can take place in a sealed envelope, provided the trustee knows it contains the terms of the trust (*Re Keen* (1939)), in this case it will be ineffective as the letter is given a day after the will. It could be argued that this is *de minimis* and is effectively contemporaneous with the will. If all the terms were communicated on November 29 then the letter will satisfy LPA 1925, s.53(1)(b) which stipulates that trust of land must be evidenced (*i.e.* need not be made) in writing.

Jane can accept the trust by implication. It appears that there is no conflict between the will and the terms of the trust that are alleged to have been communicated on November 29. If, however, the real communication is by letter contemporaneous with the will then there is a conflict, for the trusts had not at that stage been communicated. Thus Nathan could not claim the property.

Nathan has purported to declare a gift of his expectancy under Malcolm's will. According to *Re Ellenborough* (1903) a declaration of non-existent property is void. However, if there is a valid half secret trust in his favour, he may be able to establish that he had an interest in the property from the date of the communication of the trust to Jane. This follows from another unsatisfactory case *Re Gardner (No.2)* (1923), where a gift to a beneficiary was held not to lapse even though the beneficiary died before the testator (though after the communication of the trust to the trustee). Even if it is accepted that secret and half secret trusts operate *dehors* the will, it is difficult to understand how the trust could be properly constituted before the death of the testator. Nathan can declare a trust orally of the £100,000 but the declaration respecting Dunborin would have to be evidenced in writing to satisfy the LPA 1925, s.53(1)(b). It might also be argued that the declaration was in fact a disposition of an equitable interest which needs to be made, not merely evidenced, in writing and this section would apply not only to the house but also to the money. In *Grainge v Wilberforce* (1889) it was said that where there is a sub-trust, the original beneficiary will disappear from the picture and the property will be held by the original trustee direct for the beneficiary of the sub-trust. It appears from the facts given that Nathan had no active duties to perform as a trustee so it might indeed be held to be a disposition.

The parties should therefore be advised that it is possible that there was no valid half secret trust so that Jane should hold the property for Hanbury. However even if there were a valid trust for Nathan it is highly unlikely, due to the nature of Nathan's interest and the lack of formalities, that the National Vegetarian Council could claim the property. It is most likely that Nathan's estate would benefit.

Question 5

Tom is a trustee of property for his nephew Nick who is 10. The trust property consisted of £50,000 in cash, some Government securities, and some valuable antiques.

Tom gave the £50,000 to his daughter Bella. She had no knowledge of the trust. She used the money to buy a house, which she redecorated. She has just resold the house for £70,000.

Tom has sold the antiques to a bona fide purchaser for value without notice of the trust and spent the proceeds on a holiday in Greece.

The income from the Government securities was credited to
Tom's bank account. He opened the account in May this year,
which shows the following transactions. Credits May 2: £400
(income from Nick's trust), May 4: £200 (income from another
trust), May 6: £100 (money Tom won on a horse), June 10: £200
(further horse winnings). Debits May 10: £100 money withdrawn, May 15, a further £100 withdrawn.

Advise Nick's mother.

Answer

As a trustee, Tom is under a duty to conserve the trust assets. If
he is in breach of trust, the beneficiary can sue him for the loss
to the trust estate. Where Tom has insufficient assets of his own,
or where the property has increased in value, it will be in the
interests of the beneficiary to recover the actual trust funds or
the property into which they have been converted.

Nick cannot follow the property according to the common-
law rules as he has only an equitable interest under a trust.
(Even if he had a legal interest he could not follow his property
into a mixed fund.) He can, however, trace the property in
equity if three conditions are fulfilled. First there has to be an
initial fiduciary relationship. This condition is fulfilled as there is
a trust. Tom is holding the property on behalf of his nephew
Nick. Secondly the property must be traceable, and thirdly
tracing must not produce an inequitable result. It is necessary to
consider these two conditions when dealing with the separate
items.

As Bella was not aware that the money was trust money and
as she did not give any consideration she is an innocent
volunteer. This means she is not liable as a constructive trustee
but it is not considered inequitable to trace the trust funds in her
hands. Nick is entitled to the £70,000 representing the original
£50,000 and the increase in its value. If, however, Bella had
spent substantial sums on the property she would be entitled to
share *pari passu* (rateably) in the increase in value as well as
reclaiming her initial expenditure (*Re Diplock* (1948)).

It is not equitable to trace against a bona fide purchaser for
value who has no notice of the trust. The proceeds, having been
spent, are irrevocable. The property no longer exists and so
cannot be traced (*Re Diplock* (1948)).

Money deposited in bank accounts is traceable according to
special rules. Where a trustee mixes trust money with his own

he is presumed to pay out his own money first rather than to have committed a breach of trust *(Re Hallet's Estate* (1880)). Thus the £100 paid out on May 10 would be taken to be the £100 he paid in on May 6 as a result of his horse-winnings. When he made the second withdrawal on May 15 he no longer had any money of his own in the account. Nor would the payment in on June 10 be taken to replace the trust moneys unless that was Tom's specific intention *(Roscoe v Winder* (1915)). Tom therefore has withdrawn £100 of trust money. Though it might be fairer that the loss should be borne by the two trust funds rateably this is not the law. The rule in *Clayton's Case* (1816), first in, first out, will be applied. In other words the withdrawal is deemed to be made from the £400 representing the interest on Nick's funds. The rule, which originated as a rule of commercial convenience, results in Nick's trust bearing the whole of the loss while the other funds remain intact.

Nick's mother should be advised that Nick will be entitled to trace the £70,000 and the £300 in the bank account. A personal action could be brought against Tom for the dissipation of the other moneys. She should also be advised to apply for Tom to be removed from the trust under the court's inherent jurisdiction.

Question 6(a)

Chive told Garlic that he wanted her to hold some shares in a private company on trust for Marjoram and Thyme. He then telephoned the director of the company asking him to carry out the details of the transfer.

The next day Chive was involved in an accident at his home. Marjoram and Thyme visited him. He told them of his conversation with Garlic and handed the share certificates to them. Unexpectedly, Chive died that night from his injuries. Garlic is the executor of Chive's will.

Advise Marjoram and Thyme.

Question 6(b)

Parsley covenanted with Dill and Mint that he would transfer Cabbage-Patch to them to hold on trust for his co-habitee, Rosemary, and their child Basil. His will, made earlier, had left all his property to Sage. At his death Cabbage-Patch had not been transferred.

Advise Rosemary.

Answer (a)

In order to be enforceable a trust must be properly constituted either by the settlor making a declaration of trust or by transferring the trust property to trustees. A trust of shares can be declared orally but an ineffective transfer will not be construed as a declaration (*Jones v Lock* (1865)).

Chive has purported to transfer the shares to Garlic. He has not done so effectively. As Turner L.J. said in *Milroy v Lord* (1862) "there is no equity . . . to perfect an imperfect gift". To transfer shares a share transfer form must be executed and the shares registered by the company in the name of the transferee. If, however, the transferor has done everything he needs to do, for example executing the transfer, but the effectiveness of the gift depends on a third party the gift will not fail (*Re Rose* (1952)). Where the transferor needs to take some further steps, like obtaining Treasury consent, the gift will not be effective (*Re Fry* (1946)). On the facts Chive has merely made a telephone call which is clearly not sufficient.

Where a donor makes a gift in contemplation of imminent death, *a donatio mortis causa*, equity may in some circumstances perfect what would otherwise be an imperfect gift. The gift must have been made in contemplation of imminent death (*Duffield v Elwes* (1827)). Here Chive died but he did not make the gift because he expected to die for his immediate death was unanticipated.

Another difficulty for Marjoram and Thyme if they want to enforce the gift is that only certain property is capable of being the subject-matter of *a donatio mortis causa*. It may be that shares cannot be (see *Ward v Turner* (1752)) and *Re Weston* (1902), but contrast *Staniland v Willott* (1852)). Accepting that shares are capable of being the subject-matter of *a donatio mortis causa*, the handing over of the share certificates (even without a completed form of transfer) would amount to sufficient delivery of the gift.

Marjoram and Thyme may be more successful under an extension of the rule in *Strong v Bird* (1874). Where there is a continuing intention by the donor to make a gift and the property has been lawfully vested in the donee in another capacity, as where he is the personal representative of the deceased, the gift will be effective. In this case, however, Garlic is not the intended beneficiary but only the trustee. Nevertheless in *Re Ralli's Will Trust* (1964), this principle was extended to a situation where a trustee obtained the legal estate in another capacity, namely as sole surviving trustee under a will. Thus Garlic will be bound to hold the shares for Marjoram and Thyme. This is of course a quite fortuitous result as Chive might easily have appointed someone other than Garlic as executor.

Answer (b)

This is another example of an incompletely constituted trust. Parsley has not transferred the subject matter of the trust to the trustees but has merely covenanted to do so.

Incompletely constituted trusts cannot be enforced by volunteers. Rosemary and Basil gave no consideration and there is no question of marriage consideration for Rosemary and Parsley are not married nor is there any evidence of a settlement made in contemplation of marriage.

There is of course a contract between Parsley and the trustees. The trustees could sue for breach of contract, but as they have not lost anything their damages will be purely nominal. Moreover the court in *Re Pryce* (1917) refused to authorise the trustees to sue and in *Re Kay's Settlement* (1939) and *Re Cook's Settlement* (1965) the trustees were directed not to sue. The only case to the contrary is *Re Cavendish-Browne's Settlement* (1916) where trustees did sue for damages and succeeded. The damages were a sum equivalent to the value of the property comprised in the covenant and it was held that the money received by way of damages should be held on the trusts of the settlement. The case concerned specific land in Canada and so it could be argued that it could apply to Cabbage-Patch that is specific existing property.

There is no question of Dill and Mint obtaining specific performance as they did not give any consideration.

Rosemary and Basil might allege that there was a properly constituted trust of *a chose in action*, namely the benefit of the covenant to settle the property. This was found to be the case in *Fletcher v Fletcher* (1844), but it is unlikely today that the facts would support the intention to create a trust of the covenant.

Rosemary should be advised that she has not a strong case for claiming Cabbage-Patch. If she does not succeed the property will pass to Sage under Parsley's will.

Question 7

In 1977, Baker purchased two adjoining plots of land: Homeacre, costing £10,000, and Backacre, costing £8,000. Baker told
his solicitor that he wanted Homeacre conveyed "into the care
of" his son, Lewis, and this was done. Lewis then built a house
on Homeacre at a cost of £15,000 and, upon its completion in
1978, Baker said that Lewis could take over Backacre as a part of
the garden. In reliance upon this, Lewis constructed a swimming pool in Backacre at a cost of £2,000.

In 1980, Baker executed a will by which, after appointing
Lewis as his sole executor, he specifically devised Backacre to
Charles and left all his residuary estate to Gertrude. Baker died
earlier this year.

Advise Lewis, as executor, who is entitled to Homeacre and
Backacre.

Answer

As an executor Lewis has a fiduciary duty towards all the
persons entitled to his father's estate. He would be in breach of
that duty if he simply claimed Homeacre and Backacre as his
own. As regards Homeacre he obtained the legal estate by the
conveyance in 1977, but it may be that he held the property on a
resulting trust for his father. He has had the beneficial use of
Backacre since 1978 but not the legal title.

Homeacre

Where property is conveyed into the name of one person, the
purchase money being provided by another, there is a presumption that the legal owner will hold the property on a resulting
trust for the person who provided the money (*Dyer v Dyer*
(1788)). Thus it might be that Lewis is holding the property on a
resulting trust for Baker. Support is given to the presumption by
the instruction given by Baker to his solicitor that he wanted the
property conveyed "into the care of" his son Lewis. On the
other hand there is another presumption, the presumption of
advancement, which arises where the person providing the
money is under an equitable obligation to support the person to
whom the property is conveyed. So if the person who provides
the money is the husband or father or stands in *loco parentis* to

the person to whom the legal estate is conveyed then it will be presumed that a gift was intended. This presumption in turn can be rebutted as where the son is a solicitor or the parents are elderly and are not minded to deal with their own affairs (*Garrett v Wilkinson* (1848)).

In this case it seems likely that a gift was intended by Baker to his son, Lewis. Lewis presumably thought so otherwise he would not have spent money building a house on the property. Even if there was not an immediate gift, in 1977 he has acted to his detriment in the expectation of acquiring some interest in the property and so should be entitled under the principle of proprietary estoppel *(Inwards v Baker* (1965)). Though the court has a wide discretion in the remedies it can give for such an interest the most appropriate would seem to confirm that Lewis has a fee simple absolute (*Pascoe v Turner* (1979)).

Further evidence that a gift was intended is found in the will itself. Baker makes no specific devise of Homeacre. The reason, no doubt, is that he considered he had already disposed of Homeacre in 1977.

Backacre

Backacre has been left to Charles. This might indicate that Baker did not intend to make a gift of the property to Lewis in 1978. The legal estate remained with Baker till his death. If there was a continuing intention by Baker to make a gift to Lewis then the appointment of Lewis as executor might perfect an imperfect gift under the rule in *Strong v Bird* (1874). As executor Lewis will have the legal estate vested in him. The fact that Baker stood by while Lewis constructed a swimming pool might be evidence of a continuing intention to make a gift. If not Lewis might be able to claim an interest under the principles of proprietary estoppel as explained in relation to Homeacre. However, considering the relative value of the property and the cost of the swimming pool, which does not necessarily enhance the value of the property, the court might consider it appropriate merely to give Lewis a charge on the property for £2,000.

Lewis should be advised that he has a good claim to Homeacre but that it is unlikely that he will be entitled to Backacre.

Question 8(a)

The Oxford Young Methodists Association (an unincorporated body) decided to launch an appeal to provide funds to further its youth work "amongst youngsters who are, or are likely to become, Methodists in the Oxford area". Money is raised through collecting boxes, discos and raffles, in part, and by requiring the parents of those youngsters using its present facilities to pay 50p each week on behalf of their child(ren).

The association was recently overjoyed to receive on trust a legacy from Don of £1,000,000 "to be used to build facilities for the Oxford Young Methodists Association to use in their work, especially youth clubs".

Advise the association as to whether Don's gift will be a valid trust for a purpose.

Question 8(b)

During the building projects the Oxford Young Methodists Association is subsumed into the South East Region Young Methodists Association. Having met all its liabilities, the Oxford Association's bank account has a surplus of £100,000 which the Crown claims as *bona vacantia*.

Advise the members of the Oxford Association, all of whom were parents of the children using its facilities.

Answer (a)

Trusts must have a human beneficiary. Purposes trusts, with a few exceptions, are invalid unless they are charitable. It could be argued that this is a charitable trust under the fourth head given by Lord Macnaghten in *Pemsel's Case* (1891), being a trust for purposes beneficial to the community. The Recreational Charities Act 1958 provides that the provision of facilities for recreation and leisure-time occupation in the interests of social welfare can be charitable. Facilities needed for youth are specifically covered. However a trust must still be for the public benefit. Here the money is for an association that provides for only a small section of society, a class within a class, namely Methodists in the Oxford area. It would therefore fail *(Re Baddeley* (1955)). This part of the decision is not affected by the Recreational Charities Act 1958.

A non-charitable purpose trust is *prima facie* void *(Leahy v Att-Gen* (1959)). One of the reasons for this is that there is no one to enforce the trust. However, where property was given to trustees for the provision of a sports ground for employees, it was considered that the employees had a sufficient interest to be able to enforce the trust *(Re Denley* (1969)). Here the "youngsters" or their parents would have a sufficient interest to enforce the trust. Another problem with purpose trusts is that the capital can be tied up forever, and thus offend the rule against inalienability. This problem was avoided in *Re Recher* (1972) by holding that the gift was intended to be an accretion to the funds of the society, which were subject to the members' control. They could therefore divide the capital among themselves at any time. In this case Don has specifically stated that he wants the money to be used for building facilities. In a similar case, *Re Lipinski* (1976), where money was given to the Hull Judean (Maccabi) Association for the construction of buildings the court was able to hold that the gift was nevertheless for the members of the association.

Provided that the members of the Oxford Young Methodists Association control the funds or can change their constitution so that they can do so *(cf. Re Grant's Will Trusts* (1980) where the constitution precluded such control and the constitution could not be altered without the approval of an outside body) then Don's gift will be a valid trust for the members of the association.

Answer (b)

Where an unincorporated association is dissolved there is often a problem about surplus funds. The South Eastern Region Young Methodists Association cannot claim the money unless the constitution of the Oxford Association provides for the money to be used for the purposes of any similar association.

There are three other possible claimants to the surplus funds; those who provided the money, the Crown, and the members of the association.

Where property is given on trust for a purpose which is no longer feasible or is surplus to requirements there is sometimes held to be a resulting trust in favour of those providing the money. In *Re Gillingham Bus Disaster Fund* (1959), money was collected for the victims of a road accident. Much more money was collected than was necessary. It was held that each donor had an interest under a resulting trust. This is clearly inconvenient where it is impossible to trace the donors. On the facts of the question, there would be no difficulty about Don's legacy which could be held on a resulting trust for his estate *(Re West*

Sussex (1930)), but there would be problems about money received from the general public through collecting boxes and discos.

A more practical solution is to regard money raised in such a way as an outright gift. Indeed where money is paid for raffles and discos those who pay have received what they contracted for *(Re West Sussex* (1930)). Thus on the dissolution of the association the property no longer has an owner and would go to the Crown as *bona vacantia*.

The modern approach is to distribute the assets of an association on dissolution among its existing members *(Re Bucks Constabulary Fund (No.2)* (1979)). Although the case did not involve a legacy, the dicta by Walton J. in *Re Recher* (1972) is wide enough to preclude a resulting trust whatever the source of the money. So in the absence of rules to the contrary the surplus funds might be distributed to the members of the Oxford Association at the time of its dissolution. Any parents who have ceased to be members would not be entitled to claim *(Re Sick and Funeral Society of St John's Sunday School, Golcar* (1973)). On the other hand, Don's estate might claim the legacy on the basis of a resulting trust, relying on the recent case of *Davis v Richards & Wallington Industries Ltd* (1991). In any event the members of the association should be advised to contest the claim of the Crown.

INDEX